Rosemary and Michael Gre and are grateful for the privi in Christian ministry. This ye wedding anniversary. They worked together at Regent College, Vancouver, and later at Holy Trinity Church, Raleigh, North Carolina, but now live in Abingdon near Oxford.

Rosemary has written notes for the Bible Reading Fellowship for 25 years and is the author of the valuable book on pastoral care, *God's Catalyst*.

Michael is a Classics and New Testament scholar, with a doctorate in divinity, and is also an evangelist. He was principal of St John's School of Mission, Nottingham, has served on the faculty at Wycliffe Hall, Oxford, and Regent College, Vancouver, has taught in three universities and written more than fifty books, most recently *Jesus for Sceptics* and *When God Breaks In*. He was Rector of St Aldate's, Oxford, for more than a decade and now conducts student missions in universities in the UK and Europe.

IN TOUCH WITH GOD

Advent meditations on biblical prayers

Michael and Rosemary Green

First published in Great Britain in 2017

Society for Promoting Christian Knowledge
36 Causton Street
London SW1P 4ST
www.spck.org.uk

British Library Cataloguing-in-Publication Data
A catalogue record for this book is available from the British Library

ISBN 978–0–281–07812–7
eBook ISBN 978–0–281–07813–4

1 3 5 7 9 10 8 6 4 2

Typeset by Fakenham Prepress Solutions, Fakenham, Norfolk NR21 8NN
Manufacture managed by Jellyfish
Printed in Great Britain by CPI

eBook by Fakenham Prepress Solutions

Produced on paper from sustainable forests

Contents

Contents

Foreword

'You know what time it is, how it is now the moment for you to wake from sleep. For salvation is nearer to us now than when we became believers' (Romans 13.11).

The great Advent call proclaims that Jesus is coming back and bids us to get ready. Yet we get so caught up with the hustle and bustle of our preparations for Christmas that we don't know where to start with the most important preparation of all – getting ready to welcome Jesus into our world and our lives.

Fortunately Michael and Rosemary Green have provided us with a practical and highly accessible book to help us do just that. Their book *In Touch with God* contains daily reflections for Advent from the Old and New Testaments, based on the prayers of many people in the Bible, starting with God's call to Abram right through to the response of the shepherds and angels to the birth of Jesus.

These daily reflections, each based on a biblical passage, introduce us to very varied characters in the Bible, the issues they faced and the prayers they uttered in response to God's call in their lives. Each passage is followed by a 'Thought for the day' and a 'Prayer for the day', both of which give us food for reflection and meditation to link what we have read to our own experience and the challenges we are facing in our own lives.

This thought-provoking writing will help each of us to deepen our knowledge of God and our relationship with him during the course of our Advent journey. Michael and Rosemary Green draw on a lifetime's experience, he as an evangelist and she as a pastor. They help us to reflect on what it means for us to welcome Jesus afresh as our Saviour and Lord.

I hope you will enjoy my Advent Book for 2017 and that it will help you in your journey of faith.

John Sentamu,
Archbishop of York

Introduction

The vision for this book came from SPCK. We were kindly invited to write on some of the great prayers of the Old Testament. Rosemary has for many years been writing notes for the Bible Reading Fellowship and they have been much appreciated. Michael's expertise is as a New Testament scholar. So, for both of us, it was a new experience to feed on and then attempt to write about the prayers of the Old Testament, and we have loved it. We hope you will enjoy it, too.

Why, you might ask, should we bother with the prayers of the Old Testament? Two reasons spring to mind. The first is that these prayers are superb in their variety, the personalities of their different authors and the circumstances in which they wrote. They are also, however, united in their conviction that God is real, his ears are open to our prayers and he longs to bring us rescue, but our wrongdoing cuts us off from him and needs to be cleared away by genuine repentance. These people of the Old Testament worshipped the same God as we do, and although they knew less about him before the coming of Jesus, they seem to have been more diligent in their prayers than many of us. Daniel, for example, busy prime minister though he was, followed the regular Jewish habit of praying three times a day.

The other reason is that the Old Testament was the Bible of Jesus. He believed that it was the very word of God, it was fully inspired and not one 'jot or tittle' would fall from it until all it predicted was accomplished. He soaked himself in Scripture and particularly the psalms. We learn that Jesus went 'as his custom was' to the synagogue to worship, and there he would have used liturgical prayer in company with others. We read that he went out early in the morning to pray in solitude and silence, like many of his Old Testament predecessors. In facing his temptations he used quotations from the Old Testament as weapons. He quoted Psalm 110 several times, and saw his own role – of being the Davidic Messiah, a high priest like Melchizedek and achieving victory over his foes – foreshadowed in this psalm, which also became a favourite among his followers. He cleansed the Temple of its money-lenders and restored its proper role as 'a house of prayer'. He told his priestly accusers that the day would come when they would see the Son of Man sitting at the right hand of God, as Daniel had predicted. He quoted Psalm 22 as he was in agony on the cross: 'My God, my God, why have you forsaken me?' and, as he passed away, he quoted Psalm 31: 'Into your hand I commit my spirit.'

From first to last we see how Jesus immersed himself in the writings of these Old Testament saints, particularly the psalms and Isaiah. Indeed, the New Testament would be shredded if we extracted from it all the Old Testament references and quotations. If it was necessary and profitable for Jesus, it should surely be no less so for us. If we read these prayers slowly and thoughtfully and use them in our own intercessions this Advent, they will deepen our spiritual lives and bring us closer to our Lord.

Michael and Rosemary Green

1

Abraham: God's promises in our despair

After these things the word of the LORD came to Abram in a vision, 'Do not be afraid, Abram, I am your shield; your reward shall be very great.' But Abram said, 'O Lord GOD, what will you give me, for I continue childless, and the heir of my house is Eliezer of Damascus?' And Abram said, 'You have given me no offspring, and so a slave born in my house is to be my heir.' But the word of the LORD came to him, 'This man shall not be your heir; no one but your very own issue shall be your heir.' He brought him outside and said, 'Look towards heaven and count the stars, if you are able to count them.' Then he said to him, 'So shall your descendants be.' And he believed the LORD; and the LORD reckoned it to him as righteousness.

(Genesis 15.1–6)

There was once a professor of church history who began his inaugural lecture with a statement which stupefied his class. He said, 'Church history does not begin with Jesus. It begins with Abraham.'

Actually the professor was quite right. God is consistent. His approach to his people under the old covenant is exactly the same as his approach under the new. Two words are central: grace and faith. God approaches us in sheer grace, utter undeserved love; and our response is not to try to earn his favour or pay him back for it, but to trust him gratefully. That is why verse 6 is so important if we are to understand the message of the entire Bible.

Think of it! Abraham (or Abram as he was called then) was not just any old shepherd. He lived nearly 2,000 years before Christ and was a wealthy member of one of the most advanced civilizations in the world, Ur of the Chaldees. If you want to get a glimpse of its splendour, make time to go and see some of its artefacts in the British Museum. God, however, had made it plain to him that he should leave it all behind and start out on a journey with no fixed destination (12.1–4). Amazingly this astonishing man obeyed: 'Abram went, as the LORD had told him' (12.4). But God never asks us to do something very difficult without making us a promise of his support. And the promise he made to Abraham was astounding; its shadow reached over the whole Bible (12.2).

> I will make of you a great nation, and I will bless you, and make your name great, so that you will be a blessing. I will bless those who bless you, and the one who curses

you I will curse; and in you all the families of the earth shall be blessed.

Abram had a lot of difficult experiences after that, and he made serious mistakes. Worst of all he found that he and Sarah could not have children: she was barren. No wonder Genesis 15.1 shows his discouragement and fear that the promise could not possibly come true. After all, he had no children, so how on earth could any people, let alone all the people of the earth, be blessed through him? He could see no answer to this question and so he poured his heart out before the Lord (15.2–3).

'O Lord GOD, what will you give me, for I continue childless, and the heir of my house is Eliezer of Damascus?' And Abram said, 'You have given me no offspring, and so a slave born in my house is to be my heir.'

You can almost hear the doubt, fear and despair in those words. Have I left Ur's ease for the desert near Sodom for this? There seems to be no way in which God can possibly be true to his promise! Have I made the mistake of my life, leaving Ur?

God met Abram in his despair. Gently, firmly, he told him (15.4–6):

'This man shall not be your heir; no one but your very own issue shall be your heir.' He brought him outside and

3

said, 'Look towards heaven and count the stars, if you are able to count them.' Then he said to him, 'So shall your descendants be.' And he believed the LORD; and the LORD reckoned it to him as righteousness.

What a statement! Trusting God in the dark is the way to get right with him. There is nothing we can do to *earn* a right standing with God, but he is prepared to give it to us, as he did to Abram, if we trust him. His grace, our faith – the path to getting right with God.

And of course it all came good. Abram and Sarah had the promised child, and through him the whole tribe which became Israel gradually took shape. But that was not enough. That was not worldwide in its scope, as the promise had indicated. The centrepiece of that offspring was Jesus of Nazareth, and through him the divine grace–faith reciprocal has spread to the whole world, as the New Testament loves to stress (e.g. Galatians 3.5–9).

Thought for the day

When doubt and despair strike, hold fast to some promise of God.

Prayer for the day

Lord, help me, like Abraham, to trust you when I cannot see the way ahead.

MG

4

2

Jacob: broken and remade

The same night he got up and took his two wives, his two maids, and his eleven children, and crossed the ford of the Jabbok. He took them and sent them across the stream, and likewise everything that he had. Jacob was left alone; and a man wrestled with him until daybreak. When the man saw that he did not prevail against Jacob, he struck him on the hip socket; and Jacob's hip was put out of joint as he wrestled with him. Then he said, 'Let me go, for the day is breaking.' But Jacob said, 'I will not let you go, unless you bless me.' So he said to him, 'What is your name?' And he said, 'Jacob.' Then the man said, 'You shall no longer be called Jacob, but Israel, for you have striven with God and with humans, and have prevailed.' Then Jacob asked him, 'Please tell me your name.' But he said, 'Why is it that you ask my name?' And there he blessed him. So Jacob called the place Peniel, saying, 'For I have seen God face to face, and yet my life is preserved.' The sun rose upon him as he passed Peniel, limping because of his hip. Therefore to this day the Israelites do not eat the thigh muscle that is on the hip socket, because he struck Jacob on the hip socket at the thigh muscle.

(Genesis 32.22–32)

We tend to imagine that if some famous character appears in the Bible, he or she must be rather saintly. This is of course far from the truth. Scripture was written for our learning, we are told, and sometimes we learn most from bad examples. Jacob was, quite frankly, a rogue, a very nasty piece of work. He was as unlike his godly grandfather Abraham as could be. He was a liar, a thief, a self-serving schemer and a coward. And yet in God's mercy he became one of the godly founders of the people of Israel. God loves to take failures and make them saints. The stages in Jacob's transformation still speak to us today, and we see most of them in this short passage.

First, Jacob had hit rock bottom. He had lost hope. This was the night before he met Esau, whom he had cheated. He was convinced Esau was going to kill him. As he lay down and tried to sleep he probably said to himself, 'Jacob, you are finished. All your crooked schemes have come to nothing. Tomorrow you meet Esau who is pursuing you with 400 men.' In a word, he came to see that the life he had lived for the past 50 years had brought disaster. His wily schemes had collapsed in ruins. His life seemed to be at an end. 'Jacob was left alone.'

But often man's extremity is God's opportunity. And in this amazing story we find God wrestling Jacob into submission. It was a theophany. Jacob did not know God was facing him in this man who would not disclose his name, but he was quite clear about it by the end of the struggle: 'Jacob called the place Peniel, saying, "For I have seen God face to face, and yet my life is preserved."' It was a night-long struggle: it often is when God comes and wrestles for supremacy in our lives. We are so reluctant to surrender our proud ego to the love that will not let us go. Jacob would not give in. Then God touched the hollow of his thigh, putting it out of joint, and the wrestling match was over.

The thigh muscle is probably the strongest in the body. Jacob's will have been well developed because, throughout his life, whenever he was in trouble he ran away! That was his solution to every problem. His point of greatest physical strength was his point of greatest spiritual weakness. But not after that night. Never again could he escape from situations by running. He limped for the rest of his life. He had to rely on God. A very painful lesson, but we all have to learn it. God's strength is only available to us when we acknowledge our own weakness. St Paul made the same discovery (2 Corinthians 12.9ff.).

Notice that earlier in the chapter Jacob had made an eloquent prayer (Genesis 32.9–12). He admitted his unworthiness. He acknowledged God's faithfulness to him. He claimed God's promise. There was nothing wrong with that prayer. But all the time he was his own man, dealing with God on his own terms. He had to be broken if God was truly to bless him. And when he acknowledged defeat and cried to God for blessing, he found that defeat was turned into victory. His conqueror gave him a new name. No longer Jacob the schemer, but Israel the prince with God. And despite many ups and downs his subsequent life showed the fruit of that wrestling match.

Thought for the day

I may need God to break me if he is to remake me.

Prayer for the day

I will not let you go unless you bless me.

MG

3

Moses: meet God alone

Now Moses used to take the tent and pitch it outside the camp, far off from the camp; he called it the tent of meeting. And everyone who sought the LORD would go out to the tent of meeting, which was outside the camp. Whenever Moses went out to the tent, all the people would rise and stand, each of them, at the entrance of their tents and watch Moses until he had gone into the tent. When Moses entered the tent, the pillar of cloud would descend and stand at the entrance of the tent, and the LORD would speak with Moses. When all the people saw the pillar of cloud standing at the entrance of the tent, all the people would rise and bow down, all of them, at the entrance of their tents. Thus the LORD used to speak to Moses face to face, as one speaks to a friend. Then he would return to the camp; but his young assistant, Joshua son of Nun, would not leave the tent.

Moses said to the LORD, 'See, you have said to me, "Bring up this people"; but you have not let me know whom you will send with me. Yet you have said, "I know you by name, and you have also found favour in my sight." Now if I have found favour in your sight, show me your ways, so that I may know you and find favour in your sight. Consider too that this nation is your people.' He said, 'My presence will go with you, and I will give you rest.' And he said to him, 'If your presence will not go, do not carry us up from here. For how shall it be known that I have found favour in your sight, I and your people, unless you go with us? In this way, we shall be distinct, I and your people, from every people on the face of the earth.'

The LORD said to Moses, 'I will do the very thing that you have asked; for you have found favour in my sight, and I know you by name.'　　　　　(Exodus 33.7–17)

In the critical North African campaign of the Second World War, General Montgomery took half an hour in his tent every day when it was well known that he was not to be disturbed. He was a Christian, and he used this time to re-establish his contact with God. He was not the first to have this idea. Jesus encouraged his friends, when they prayed, to go into a room and shut the door so as to have an undisturbed time with God (Matthew 6.6). Moses had the same idea, more than 1,000 years earlier. He had a tent called 'the tent of meeting', which was erected some distance outside the camp of the Israelites while they were journeying through the deserts of the Sinai peninsula. He went there to pray. We all need to find a place where for a short while we can be undisturbed, alone with God, on a daily basis. And we read these marvellous words, 'the LORD used to speak to Moses face to face, as one speaks to a friend' (verse 11). That was the secret of Moses' success, as it was of Montgomery's. Both of them found a place where they could be alone with God, temporarily shutting out the pressures of the day. It was the still small space at the heart of a very demanding life. And Moses' life was certainly that. He was the natural, spiritual and military leader of this refugee nation. An enormous amount depended on him. And he depended on God.

Look at this magnificent prayer again. Aware as he is of the immense responsibility of leading this difficult and apostate people, Moses' heart cries out for companionship, because leadership is lonely work. In the past he had made a similar cry, and God had answered it by providing Aaron to be his close confidant (4.14). But our earthly companions, however close, can fail us, and Aaron had just failed comprehensively, as he led the people in building the golden calf. For that reason God does not offer Moses a human companion in answer to his prayer, but someone much better, someone ultimate. He says, 'My presence will go with you, and I will give you rest.' God would not fail Moses, as Aaron had.

Moses is not prepared to take this responsibility of leadership further if God does not go with him, guide him, strengthen him and give him peace of mind. He wants to make very sure, so he repeats his request, perhaps somewhat peevishly: 'If your presence will not go, do not carry us up from here.' And God underlines his gracious offer of support. 'I will do the very thing that you have asked; for you have found favour in my sight, and I know you by name.' No more complaints after that! When God calls us to any project, he promises to go with us. Think of that similar New Testament promise:

> Be content with what you have; for he has said, 'I will never leave you or forsake you.' So we can say with confidence, 'The Lord is my helper; I will not be afraid. What can anyone do to me?' (Hebrews 13.5–6)

God plus one believer is always a majority.

There are other encouragements in this prayer. 'Now if I have found favour in your sight, show me your ways, so that I may know you and find favour in your sight.' Isn't it amazing that God Almighty can be pleased with human beings like us? Isn't it encouraging that he knows us by name (verse 17)? Take that encouragement into today!

Thought for the day

I need to find a place apart, a 'tent of meeting'.

Prayer for the day

Lord, may your presence go with me today whatever my circumstances, and may I so live that you can be pleased with me.

MG

4

Hannah: prayer, faith and faithfulness

There was a certain man of Ramathaim, a Zuphite from the hill country of Ephraim, whose name was Elkanah son of Jeroham son of Elihu son of Tohu son of Zuph, an Ephraimite. He had two wives; the name of one was Hannah, and the name of the other Peninnah. Peninnah had children, but Hannah had no children.

Now this man used to go up year by year from his town to worship and to sacrifice to the LORD of hosts at Shiloh, where the two sons of Eli, Hophni and Phinehas, were priests of the LORD. On the day when Elkanah sacrificed, he would give portions to his wife Peninnah and to all her sons and daughters; but to Hannah he gave a double portion, because he loved her, though the LORD had closed her womb. Her rival used to provoke her severely, to irritate her, because the LORD had closed her womb. So it went on year after year; as often as she went up to the house of the LORD, she used to provoke her. Therefore Hannah wept and would not eat. Her husband Elkanah said to her, 'Hannah, why do you weep? Why do you not eat? Why is your heart sad? Am I not more to you than ten sons?'

After they had eaten and drunk at Shiloh, Hannah rose and presented herself before the Lord. Now Eli the priest was sitting on the seat beside the doorpost of the temple of the Lord. She was deeply distressed and prayed to the Lord, and wept bitterly. She made this vow: 'O Lord of hosts, if only you will look on the misery of your servant, and remember me, and not forget your servant, but will give to your servant a male child, then I will set him before you as a nazirite until the day of his death. He shall drink neither wine nor intoxicants, and no razor shall touch his head.'

As she continued praying before the Lord, Eli observed her mouth. Hannah was praying silently; only her lips moved, but her voice was not heard; therefore Eli thought she was drunk. So Eli said to her, 'How long will you make a drunken spectacle of yourself? Put away your wine.' But Hannah answered, 'No, my lord, I am a woman deeply troubled; I have drunk neither wine nor strong drink, but I have been pouring out my soul before the Lord. Do not regard your servant as a worthless woman, for I have been speaking out of my great anxiety and vexation all this time.' Then Eli answered, 'Go in peace; the God of Israel grant the petition you have made to him.' And she said, 'Let your servant find favour in your sight.' Then the woman went to her quarters, ate and drank with her husband, and her countenance was sad no longer.

They rose early in the morning and worshipped before the Lord; then they went back to their house at Ramah. Elkanah knew his wife Hannah, and the Lord remembered her. In due time Hannah conceived and bore a son. She named him Samuel, for she said, 'I have asked him of the LORD.' (1 Samuel 1.1–20)

Some who are reading this know first hand the pain of struggling to conceive a child, and the deep disappointment, month after month, of finding that, yet again, there is no new life. Others know the deep sadness of miscarriage, the joy of expectancy turned abruptly into loss. Others of us have not been in that place ourselves but have tried (perhaps clumsily) to enter into the deep feelings of friends in that anguish. It was harder still for women in a society where barrenness was a shame, a disgrace thought to be the mark of God withdrawing his blessing. Jacob's wife Rachel, Abram's wife Sarai, Zechariah's wife Elizabeth, all knew that stigma. For Hannah (as for Rachel) her pain was enhanced by the taunts of 'the other wife' with many children. Sadly, her husband Elkanah only added to her distress. Despite his special love for her (verse 5) he failed to understand why the lack of children mattered so much to her (verse 8). (Husbands, how well do you really listen to your wife and try to understand her feelings, even if they are not what *you* think she ought to feel?)

The family made an annual trip to Shiloh, at that time the central place for Israel's worship, where the ark of God was kept before the Temple was built in Jerusalem. It was a pilgrimage for worship and sacrifice, a journey of joy for Elkanah and Peninnah, but for Hannah a regular, dismal reminder of her childlessness. She stood and prayed in silent, tearful distress. 'Lord, if you hear my plea and give me a son, I will dedicate him to you, he will be yours for life.' Eli the priest observed her, but misinterpreted what he saw. He assumed she was drunk, and rebuked her. But all credit to him; he listened to her explanation, he understood and he gave her God's blessing. Hannah went home with the assurance of her prayer answered, and her grief lifted. Hebrews 11.1 tells us that 'faith is the assurance of things hoped for, the conviction of things not seen'. She does not appear in the writer's long list of Old Testament saints – but she certainly belongs there; Hannah was a woman of faith.

And Hannah was a woman of prayer. In the following chapter we read the outpouring of her song of praise, even after she had made the painful parting with her newly weaned son. But as she stood in the Temple, praying through her tears, there were no words spoken out loud. Her prayer was like the prayer of which Paul writes in Romans 8.26: 'The Spirit helps us in our weakness; for we do not know how to pray as we ought, but that very

Spirit intercedes with sighs too deep for words.' I have rarely known that depth of 'groaning' (to use the word the NIV uses for sighs); I only remember one occasion, as my heart ached deeply for a Christian lady who was full of bitterness about her disability.

I want to commend Hannah for another quality. She was a woman who kept her word. Many of us might pray a similar prayer: 'O God, if you will do this for me, then I promise . . .' We forget, even when he has clearly answered our prayer, but she carried through her promise to dedicate her son to the Lord, and she left him in the Temple, to serve, as she said she would. And God blessed her with three more sons and two daughters (1 Samuel 2.21).

Thought for the day

Faith in a trustworthy God can help us turn from sorrow to peace.

Prayer for the day

Father, please help me to trust your faithfulness even when life seems uncertain.

RG

5

David: success and gratitude

Then King David went in and sat before the LORD, and said, 'Who am I, O Lord GOD, and what is my house, that you have brought me thus far? And yet this was a small thing in your eyes, O Lord GOD; you have spoken also of your servant's house for a great while to come. May this be instruction for the people, O Lord GOD! And what more can David say to you? For you know your servant, O Lord GOD! Because of your promise, and according to your own heart, you have wrought all this greatness, so that your servant may know it. Therefore you are great, O LORD God; for there is no one like you, and there is no God besides you, according to all that we have heard with our ears. Who is like your people, like Israel? Is there another nation on earth whose God went to redeem it as a people, and to make a name for himself, doing great and awesome things for them, by driving out before his people nations and their gods? And you established your people Israel for yourself to be your people for ever; and you, O LORD, became their God. And now, O LORD God, as for the word that you have spoken concerning your servant and concerning his house, confirm it for ever; do as you have promised. Thus your name will be magnified for ever in the saying, "The LORD of hosts is God over Israel"; and the house of your servant David will be established before you. For you, O LORD of hosts, the God of Israel, have made this revelation to your servant, saying, "I will build you a house"; therefore your servant has found courage to pray this prayer to you. And now, O Lord GOD, you are God, and your words are true, and you have promised this good thing to your servant; now therefore may it please you to bless the house of your servant, so that it may continue for ever before you; for you, O Lord GOD, have spoken, and with your blessing shall the house of your servant be blessed for ever.'

(2 Samuel 7.18–29)

All power tends to corrupt, and absolute power tends to corrupt absolutely. We all know this is true. But David is a striking exception. He was the greatest king Israel ever had, although he had sprung from the lowliest job, a despised shepherd. He had conquered Jerusalem and brought the ark to the city. He had beaten up the Philistines and 'the LORD had given him rest from all his enemies around him' (7.1). Does he become arrogant as a lesser man might have done? No. He is embarrassed to live in his palace of cedar while the ark of God remains in a tent. He wants to build God a 'house' for the ark, the symbol of the divine presence. That is both attractive and modest. So is the prayer in 7.18ff. It is humble, trusting and full of gratitude. That is one big lesson for our prayers which David teaches us.

But Nathan the prophet receives a word from God for David (7.5–16). It is one of the most important passages in the whole Old Testament because it concerns the Temple and David's dynasty, the two institutions which were vital for Israel. God declines David's offer to build him a 'house' (i.e. temple: that task would fall to Solomon his son). Instead God would build David a 'house' (i.e. dynasty) which would last for ever. This not only points to the tremendous generosity of God, but reminds us that like David we can go about God's work the wrong way. Instead of telling him what we propose to do, we would be wise to ask what God wants us to do.

A third thing that stands out here is that God is not very interested in temples! This is made very clear in 17.6, 7. Solomon's Temple was smashed to pieces in 587 BC. Perhaps the Church needs to learn this lesson: the Lord does not live in church buildings but in the community and hearts of his followers.

By way of contrast, Judah ceased to be a kingdom in 587 BC; David's family continued but never regained the throne.

Was God's promise, to which David clung gratefully in his prayer (7.28–29), a vain hope? Not at all. As the genealogies in Matthew and Luke are intended to emphasize, Jesus, great David's greater Son, was born of his lineage and would make good the promise. Jesus' kingdom is worldwide and will never end. He is the one who (in a more profound sense than Solomon constructing the Temple) will 'build a house for my name and I will establish the throne of his kingdom for ever' (7.13). God can be trusted to keep his promises, however improbable they may seem. David glimpsed that truth: 'your words are true, and you have promised this good thing to your servant' (7.28). This gave him confidence to conclude, 'You, O Lord GOD, have spoken, and with your blessing shall the house of your servant be blessed for ever' (7.29). His kingdom is to be found among every nation, and 3,000 years after that promise to David, the kingdom of Jesus embraces a third of humanity . . . and is growing daily.

Thought for the day

Success should make me grateful, not proud.

Prayer for the day

Who am I, sovereign Lord . . . that you have brought me thus far?

MG

6

Solomon: a discerning heart

At Gibeon the LORD appeared to Solomon in a dream by night; and God said, 'Ask what I should give you.' And Solomon said, 'You have shown great and steadfast love to your servant my father David, because he walked before you in faithfulness, in righteousness, and in uprightness of heart towards you; and you have kept for him this great and steadfast love, and have given him a son to sit on his throne today. And now, O LORD my God, you have made your servant king in place of my father David, although I am only a little child; I do not know how to go out or come in. And your servant is in the midst of the people whom you have chosen, a great people, so numerous they cannot be numbered or counted. Give your servant therefore an understanding mind to govern your people, able to discern between good and evil; for who can govern this your great people?'

It pleased the Lord that Solomon had asked this. God said to him, 'Because you have asked this, and have not asked for yourself long life or riches, or for the life of your enemies, but have asked for yourself understanding to discern what is right, I now do according to your word. Indeed I give you a wise and discerning mind; no one like you has been before you and no one like you shall arise after you. I give you also what you have not asked, both riches and honour all your life; no other king shall compare with you.   (1 Kings 3.5–13)

In some circles today, particularly in the student world, Christians often conduct a simple questionnaire, with just one question. It is this: 'If there was one thing you could ask God for, what would it be?' Most of them will have no idea that this is exactly the question God himself is represented as asking Solomon 3,000 years ago (verse 5)! It was a good question then and it is a good question now because it shows up the true nature of the person being questioned.

Solomon had been co-regent in King David's later years. He had shown himself shrewd, decisive, and he was good at completing David's unfinished business after his death. Moreover his international stature was growing. He had made an alliance with the greatest power in the Middle East, Egypt, by marrying the pharaoh's daughter. The pharaoh in question was probably Simun of the Twenty-First Dynasty (978–959 BC), but in any case the marriage enormously enhanced Solomon's international reputation. He was fortunate in that David had left him at peace with neighbouring countries. For the first part of his reign he enjoyed good relations with Egypt in the south and Tyre in the north. He was threatened by no major powers. So when God asked him what he wished for, it might have been natural for him to have requested wealth, power, success, good health or long life. After all, those are the topics people most frequently pray for today. It might also have been natural for him to ask for time to reflect on such a momentous offer.

But he did neither of these things. He replied at once, and this shows not only his decisiveness but his recognition of his greatest need. He did not ask for things, but for a quality of character. That is as unusual as it is wise. After all, when we leave this life, we will not take any of the *things* that currently seem so important to us. All we will take is our character. Solomon seems to understand this. He begins his prayer not with petition at all but with gratitude to God. He follows it with proper humility, rare in a ruler: 'I am only a little child; I do not know how to go out or come in' (verse 7). Only then does he answer God's offer and turn to his request. Alas, I turn to petition too soon in my prayers, and do not give adequate space to gratitude to God and humble confession before him.

Solomon asks for a discerning heart. We would not have guessed that the self-confident young Solomon, already praised by David for his wisdom (1 Kings 2.6, 9), lacked a discerning heart. Perhaps he sensed that this was something very different from the natural shrewdness he had already displayed.

He asked for a discerning heart, but this was not for his own benefit. Most of us, if asked what one thing we would request from God, would covet something for ourselves. Not Solomon. He wanted discernment so that he could rule his people well. The Hebrew word used for 'ruling' includes the idea of judging, justice and mercy. This was particularly important in ancient society where the king was himself the final court of appeal. The ability to rule justly and defend the poor is part of the picture Isaiah gives of God's ideal ruler (Isaiah 11.3–5) and these are among the qualities we should pray for in our own rulers, 'kings and all who are in high positions' (1 Timothy 2.2).

It is encouraging to see God's immediate answer to Solomon's prayer. Not only does he give the discerning heart that Solomon asked for (and it is immediately displayed in his judgement between the two prostitutes who both claimed to be the mother of a son) but typically God gives him other blessings he had not asked for (verse 13). God loves to give his people 'abundantly far more than all we can ask or imagine' (Ephesians 3.20). That's what he is like!

Thought for the day

I am only a little child and do not know how to go out or come in.

Prayer for the day

Give me, Lord, a discerning heart.

MG

7

Elijah: God's whisper

Ahab told Jezebel all that Elijah had done, and how he had killed all the prophets with the sword. Then Jezebel sent a messenger to Elijah, saying, 'So may the gods do to me, and more also, if I do not make your life like the life of one of them by this time tomorrow.' Then he was afraid; he got up and fled for his life, and came to Beer-sheba, which belongs to Judah; he left his servant there.

But he himself went a day's journey into the wilderness, and came and sat down under a solitary broom tree. He asked that he might die: 'It is enough; now, O LORD, take away my life, for I am no better than my ancestors.' Then he lay down under the broom tree and fell asleep. Suddenly an angel touched him and said to him, 'Get up and eat.' He looked, and there at his head was a cake baked on hot stones, and a jar of water. He ate and drank, and lay down again. The angel of the LORD came a second time, touched him, and said, 'Get up and eat, otherwise the journey will be too much for you.' He got up, and ate and drank; then he went in the strength of that food for forty days and forty nights to Horeb the mount of God. At that place he came to a cave, and spent the night there.

Then the word of the LORD came to him, saying, 'What are you doing here, Elijah?' He answered, 'I have been very zealous for the LORD, the God of hosts; for the Israelites have forsaken your covenant, thrown down your altars, and killed your prophets with the sword. I alone am left, and they are seeking my life, to take it away.'

He said, 'Go out and stand on the mountain before the LORD, for the LORD is about to pass by.' Now there was a great wind, so strong that it was splitting mountains and breaking rocks in pieces before the LORD, but the LORD was not in the wind; and after the wind an earthquake, but the LORD was not in the earthquake; and after the earthquake a fire, but the LORD was not in the fire; and after the fire a sound of sheer silence. When Elijah heard it, he wrapped his face in his mantle and went out and stood at the entrance of the cave. Then there came a voice to him that said, 'What are you doing here, Elijah?' He answered, 'I have been very zealous for the LORD, the God of hosts; for the Israelites have forsaken your covenant, thrown down your altars, and killed your prophets with the sword. I alone am left, and they are seeking my life, to take it away.' Then the LORD said to him, 'Go, return on your way to the wilderness of Damascus; when you arrive, you shall anoint Hazael as king over Aram. Also you shall anoint Jehu son of Nimshi as king over Israel; and you shall anoint Elisha son of Shaphat of Abel-meholah as prophet in your place. Whoever escapes from the sword of Hazael, Jehu shall kill; and whoever escapes from the sword of Jehu, Elisha shall kill. Yet I will leave seven thousand in Israel, all the knees that have not bowed to Baal, and every mouth that has not kissed him.'

(1 Kings 19.1–18)

There is no more towering figure in the Old Testament than the prophet Elijah. Without introduction he stalks on to the stage of Scripture, accosts the evil king Ahab and tells him there will be 'neither dew nor rain these years, except at my word' (17.1). Three years later, the streams are dry, the pastures burnt up and they meet again. 'Is it you, you troubler of Israel?' asks Ahab (18.17). Truculently Elijah replies, 'I have not troubled Israel; but you have, and your father's house, because you have forsaken the commandments of the Lord and followed the Baals' (verses 18–19) – not altogether surprising since Baal was a weather god, and they were three years into a drought! Courageously Elijah throws down the gauntlet for a trial by fire. A great crowd gathers on Mount Carmel and fearlessly Elijah challenges them, 'How long will you go limping with two different opinions? If the LORD is God, follow him; but if Baal, then follow him' (verse 21).

We all know the story with its amazing outcome. Elijah is so strong in faith that he mocks his 450 opponents as they shout out to Baal for hours and slash themselves in frenzied appeals for fire. 'Surely he is a god; either he is meditating, or he has wandered away, or he is on a journey, or perhaps he is asleep and must be awakened' (verse 27). But no fire comes from the false god. How different when Elijah's turn comes. He makes it so difficult for God to show his power, by repeatedly dousing the sacrifice with gallons of water. 'Answer me, O LORD,' he cries, 'answer me, so that this people may know that you, O LORD, are God, and that you have turned their hearts back' (verse 37). Then the fire of the Lord falls, the people return to their allegiance to God, and the prophets of Baal are killed off. What a comprehensive victory!

But all too often after an exhilarating experience depression sets in. And so it is with Elijah. Terrified of Queen Jezebel, Elijah runs for his life into the desert and asks to die. 'It is enough; now, O LORD, take away my life, for I am no better than my ancestors' (19.4). It is very instructive to note how God gradually heals him, because depression is a dark cloud that can so easily envelop any one of us. Elijah is not the only one who bursts out, 'I have had enough.'

First, he needs to sleep and take proper rest after the herculean exertions of the previous days (verse 5).

Second, he needs something nourishing to eat: he probably has not had a square meal for days (verses 6–8).

Third, he needs exercise – in his case a 40-day and 40-night journey to Mount Sinai (verse 8).

But most of all he needs a new encounter with God. And this comes not in earthquake or fire but in the enigmatic phrase, 'a sound of sheer silence' (verse 12). God often reaches us in the silence and asks us what we are doing. Still discouraged, Elijah prays: 'The Israelites have forsaken your covenant, thrown down your altars, and killed your prophets with the sword. I alone am left, and they are seeking my life, to take it away' (verse 14). Typical of the depressive, Elijah forgets the victory of Mount Carmel, discounts the return of the people to God and underestimates his support network. So God tells him that he is far from a lone voice – there are 7,000 loyal servants of the Lord like him (verse 18). And now, with his depression lifted, his head cleared and his confidence in God renewed, Elijah is ready for a fresh and complex commission (verses 15, 16).

Thought for the day

Beware of the depression that can follow exhilaration. Sleep, food, exercise, time apart with God and a fresh enterprise can help a lot.

Prayer for the day

Lord, lead me to that 'sound of sheer silence' when I am discouraged, so that you can meet me there.

MG

8

Hezekiah: God can do it!

Hezekiah received the letter from the hand of the messengers and read it; then Hezekiah went up to the house of the LORD and spread it before the LORD. And Hezekiah prayed before the LORD, and said: 'O LORD the God of Israel, who are enthroned above the cherubim, you are God, you alone, of all the kingdoms of the earth; you have made heaven and earth. Incline your ear, O LORD, and hear; open your eyes, O LORD, and see; hear the words of Sennacherib, which he has sent to mock the living God. Truly, O LORD, the kings of Assyria have laid waste the nations and their lands, and have hurled their gods into the fire, though they were no gods but the work of human hands – wood and stone – and so they were destroyed. So now, O LORD our God, save us, I pray you, from his hand, so that all the kingdoms of the earth may know that you, O LORD, are God alone.'

(2 Kings 19.14–19)

The news could hardly be worse. The Assyrians had arrived to capture Jerusalem. The nearest modern parallel to the Assyrians over the 300 years of their ascendancy (c. 900–600 BC) would be the Nazis. Both had limitless

32

ambitions. Both were the most advanced military machines in the world. Both were arrogant and cruel. And both were always looking for fresh fields to conquer.

The year was 701 BC. Hezekiah was king of the little state of Judah, and we read, 'He trusted in the LORD the God of Israel; so that there was no one like him among all the kings of Judah after him, or among those who were before him' (18.5). Sennacherib, the Assyrian king, waged an incredibly successful campaign, capturing Sidon, Arvad, Byblos, Moab and Edom. He had already exacted heavy tribute from Hezekiah, and in this further campaign he destroyed 46 walled towns and many villages in Judah, and, as he put it in his own records, 'shut up Hezekiah in Jerusalem like a bird in a cage', although he did not claim to have captured the city. If you can read cuneiform you can read Sennacherib's own account of the campaigns in what is known as Taylor's Prism in the British Museum. The Bible gives no fewer than three almost identical accounts of this encounter between the king of Assyria and the king of Israel (here, 2 Chronicles 32 and Isaiah 37). It clearly made a great impression.

Why did Sennacherib not capture Jerusalem, as he had all these other cities? There seem to be two answers. The first is that when Hezekiah received the letter from Sennacherib, threatening Hezekiah and scorning his God, the first thing Hezekiah did was to go to the Temple and spread the letter before the Lord. That is an example we could well emulate when bad news strikes. He then prayed this remarkable short prayer. First, he recognized God's special relation to Judah 'enthroned above the cherubim [of the ark]', but also that he was the God 'of all the kingdoms of the earth': he saw the balance between God's immanence and transcendence. He went on to acknowledge the seriousness of the threat and the might of Assyria on the one hand, but the insult which their idolatry offered to God on the other. He asked for what seemed highly improbable – deliverance from the hand of Sennacherib. And he seems to have desired this not only for the safety of himself and his people but 'that all the kingdoms of the earth may know that you, O LORD, are God alone' (19.19). His supreme desire was the glory of the one true God, and that should be our goal in prayer, too.

He did not pray on his own. 'King Hezekiah and the prophet Isaiah son of Amoz prayed because of this and cried to heaven' (2 Chronicles 32.20). A prayer partner at such times is invaluable, and Isaiah was inspired by God to give the king assurance that his prayer was answered and the city would not fall. So it turned out. 'That very night the angel of the LORD set out and struck down one hundred and eighty-five thousand in the camp of the Assyrians; when morning dawned, they were all dead bodies. Then King Sennacherib of Assyria left [and] went home' (19.35–36). How this remarkable divine intervention took place we do not know: bubonic plague has been suggested. But this was not the only time the mighty Assyrian army had to withdraw from besieging a town. The Greek historian Herodotus tells of the siege of Pelusium when overnight a plague of mice spread everywhere among the Assyrians, chewing their bow strings, quivers and shields so that next day they were weaponless and fled, sustaining heavy losses!

Thought for the day

Nothing is impossible with God, however bleak the outlook.

Prayer for the day

When disaster strikes, teach me to bring it straight to you, to share it with a praying friend, and to expect it somehow to redound to your credit.

MG

9

Jehoshaphat: God of the unexpected

After this the Moabites and Ammonites, and with them some of the Meunites, came against Jehoshaphat for battle. Messengers came and told Jehoshaphat, 'A great multitude is coming against you from Edom, from beyond the sea; already they are at Hazazon-tamar' (that is, En-gedi). Jehoshaphat was afraid; he set himself to seek the LORD, and proclaimed a fast throughout all Judah. Judah assembled to seek help from the LORD; from all the towns of Judah they came to seek the LORD.

Jehoshaphat stood in the assembly of Judah and Jerusalem, in the house of the LORD, before the new court, and said, 'O LORD, God of our ancestors, are you not God in heaven? Do you not rule over all the kingdoms of the nations? In your hand are power and might, so that no one is able to withstand you. Did you not, O our God, drive out the inhabitants of this land before your people Israel, and give it for ever to the descendants of your friend Abraham? They have lived in it, and in it have built you a sanctuary for your name, saying, "If disaster comes upon us, the sword, judgement, or pestilence, or famine, we will stand before this house, and before you, for your name is in this house, and cry to you in our distress, and you will hear and save." See now, the people of Ammon, Moab, and Mount Seir, whom you would not let Israel invade when they came from the land of Egypt, and whom they avoided and did not destroy – they reward us by coming to drive us out of your possession that you have given us to inherit. O our God, will you not execute judgement upon them? For we are powerless against this great multitude that is coming against us. We do not know what to do, but our eyes are on you.'

Meanwhile all Judah stood before the Lord, with their little ones, their wives, and their children. Then the spirit of the Lord came upon Jahaziel son of Zechariah, son of Benaiah, son of Jeiel, son of Mattaniah, a Levite of the sons of Asaph, in the middle of the assembly. He said, 'Listen, all Judah and inhabitants of Jerusalem, and King Jehoshaphat: Thus says the Lord to you: "Do not fear or be dismayed at this great multitude; for the battle is not yours but God's. Tomorrow go down against them; they will come up by the ascent of Ziz; you will find them at the end of the valley, before the wilderness of Jeruel. This battle is not for you to fight; take your position, stand still, and see the victory of the Lord on your behalf, O Judah and Jerusalem." Do not fear or be dismayed; tomorrow go out against them, and the Lord will be with you.'

Then Jehoshaphat bowed down with his face to the ground, and all Judah and the inhabitants of Jerusalem fell down before the LORD, worshipping the LORD. And the Levites, of the Kohathites and the Korahites, stood up to praise the LORD, the God of Israel, with a very loud voice.

They rose early in the morning and went out into the wilderness of Tekoa; and as they went out, Jehoshaphat stood and said, 'Listen to me, O Judah and inhabitants of Jerusalem! Believe in the LORD your God and you will be established; believe his prophets.' When he had taken counsel with the people, he appointed those who were to sing to the LORD and praise him in holy splendour, as they went before the army, saying, 'Give thanks to the LORD, for his steadfast love endures for ever.'

As they began to sing and praise, the LORD set an ambush against the Ammonites, Moab, and Mount Seir, who had come against Judah, so that they were routed. For the Ammonites and Moab attacked the inhabitants of Mount Seir, destroying them utterly; and when they had made an end of the inhabitants of Seir, they all helped to destroy one another. When Judah came to the watch-tower of the wilderness, they looked towards the multitude; they were corpses lying on the ground; no one had escaped.   (2 Chronicles 20.1–24)

Jehoshaphat, who had succeeded his father Asa as king of Judah in about 870 BC, continued his father's reforms – spiritual, legal and military. But his marriage alliance with the Baal-worshipping king of Israel, Ahab, nearly cost him his life in battle, almost brought the Davidic line to extinction a generation later and earned him fierce words from the prophet Jehu: 'Should you help the wicked and love those who hate the LORD?' (19.2).

Now a new threat came from countries east of the Jordan. An urgent message arrived; a vast army was approaching, already only 25 miles away. Many of us would panic, call a committee meeting, summon the army generals to devise tactics. Not Jehoshaphat. He was afraid, but he did not panic. He set himself to seek God and he called the nation to join him. It reminds me of King George VI's call for a national day of prayer on 26 May 1940, when it seemed that Hitler would annihilate the British army in France. What followed were Hitler's astonishing decision to halt his Panzers; a storm in Flanders that grounded the Luftwaffe, who were strafing the retreating British forces; and an extraordinary calm in the Channel that enabled thousands of small boats to cross the sea and rescue 300,000 soldiers from the beaches. The miracle of Dunkirk was God's answer to a nation that prayed and did not panic.

So Jehoshaphat proclaimed a national fast, called the people together and led them in prayer. First he praised the God in heaven whose power over all the nations is supreme. Praise is always a good way to start our prayers.

He remembered what God had done in the past as the Israelites conquered the Promised Land and settled there, and their commitment to pray together when in trouble. (Was that part of the prayer more for the people than for God?) Then he laid out their desperate situation. 'We are powerless against this great multitude that is coming against us. We do not know what to do, but our eyes are on you' (20.12). I love his humility and his dependence on God. He trusted a faithful, powerful God to act. How often we suggest to God how he should act. We tell him what to do, how and when. Yes, it is all right to have our ideas. But how arrogant to prescribe to an all-knowing, all-wise, all-powerful God! Perhaps we add a postscript of *Deo volente* ('God willing') but it is very much an afterthought just in case we are wrong! I was deeply struck some years ago as we drove into Heathrow. The radar dishes, large curved-back rectangles, were constantly turning through 360 degrees to pick up the signals from any direction. We sometimes stand, firmly facing one way, complaining, 'Lord, why aren't you answering my prayer?' We shout so loudly we can't hear his whisper from behind. 'Turn round and see how I *am* answering.' Sometimes, in your private prayer, stand up with arms outstretched. Turn round slowly to express your openness to God. 'I don't know what to do, but my eyes are on you.'

The first part of God's answer came through a strong message of encouragement from Jahaziel. 'Do not fear or be dismayed . . . the battle is not yours but God's . . . stand still, and see the victory of the LORD on your behalf' (15–17). King and people fell prostrate to worship the Lord, while Levites and others stood to praise him loudly in song. They praised him, even before they saw his remarkable answer, which we read later in the chapter. You might like, too, to read Acts 4.23–31 – the disciples' prayer when they, too, were in a tough corner.

Thought for the day

Trust God for the unexpected. Read further in the chapter to see God's remarkable intervention.

Prayer for the day

Lord, I don't know what to do about . . . But my eyes are on you. I'm open to your answer, your ways.

RG

10

Ezra: humble repentance

O my God, I am too ashamed and embarrassed to lift my face to you, my God, for our iniquities have risen higher than our heads, and our guilt has mounted up to the heavens. From the days of our ancestors to this day we have been deep in guilt, and for our iniquities we, our kings, and our priests have been handed over to the kings of the lands, to the sword, to captivity, to plundering, and to utter shame, as is now the case. But now for a brief moment favour has been shown by the LORD our God, who has left us a remnant, and given us a stake in his holy place, in order that he may brighten our eyes and grant us a little sustenance in our slavery. For we are slaves; yet our God has not forsaken us in our slavery, but has extended to us his steadfast love before the kings of Persia, to give us new life to set up the house of our God, to repair its ruins, and to give us a wall in Judea and Jerusalem.

And now, our God, what shall we say after this? For we have forsaken your commandments, which you commanded by your servants the prophets, saying, 'The land that you are entering to possess is a land unclean with the pollutions of the peoples of the lands, with their abominations. They have filled it from end to end with their uncleanness. Therefore do not give your daughters to their sons, neither take their daughters for your sons, and never seek their peace or prosperity, so that you may be strong and eat the good of the land and leave it for an inheritance to your children for ever.' After all that has come upon us for our evil deeds and for our great guilt, seeing that you, our God, have punished us less than our iniquities deserved and have given us such a remnant as this, shall we break your commandments again and intermarry with the peoples who practise these abominations? Would you not be angry with us until you destroy us without remnant or survivor? O LORD, God of Israel, you are just, but we have escaped as a remnant, as is now the case. Here we are before you in our guilt, though no one can face you because of this.   (Ezra 9.6–15)

Three of the hardest words to utter are 'I was wrong.' Our pride makes them stick in our throat. This seems to be particularly the case with political leaders. Tony Blair lost the respect of the British people when he repeatedly refused to admit that he had been wrong to embroil the country in war with Iraq. If that is a common weakness among leaders, Ezra stands out as a shining exception.

Shortly after his conquest of Babylon, the Persian king Cyrus issued a decree (in 538 BC) allowing the Jews to return to Israel, and to restore the Temple and its fittings (Ezra 1.1ff). Not all the Jews returned, and the work was much hindered by local opposition, but by 520 BC the Temple was rebuilt after a fashion. Ezra, described in King Artaxerxes' edict as 'the priest . . . the scribe of the law of the God of heaven' (7.12), seems to have held an important post in the Babylonian courts, perhaps as a sort of Secretary of State for Jewish affairs. At all events he was sent to Jerusalem in 458 BC, together with a further wave of returning exiles: the text of the royal decree authorizing this is quoted in full (7.12–26). He was to transport valuable gifts for the Temple, to appoint magistrates and ensure that the law of the Lord and the law of the king were being observed – a delicate task since the two were not always identical!

Ezra was shocked to find extensive intermarriage between the returned Jews and the surrounding pagans.

> They have taken some of their daughters as wives for themselves and for their sons. Thus the holy seed has mixed itself with the peoples of the lands, and in this faithlessness the officials and leaders have led the way.
>
> (9.2)

Ezra at once poured out his heart in profound repentance before God. This is all the more remarkable because he had not done anything wrong himself, but he took responsibility, as a leader in the community which should have adhered to God's command but spectacularly failed to do so. He confesses the guilt of his nation down the centuries. He acknowledges that the exile was divine punishment for it. And he is heartbroken that the 'brief moment', as he calls it, when 'favour has been shown by the LORD our God, who has left us a remnant' has been put at risk, and the land polluted by intermarriage with 'the peoples who practise these abominations' (verse 14). I find Ezra's humble prayer of repentance very challenging. How much do I care about the injustice, the sexual immorality, the overflowing prisons, the grinding poverty that drives people to foodbanks, the hatred, the homelessness, the resistance against accepting refugees and the many other issues which disfigure our society? These things may not be our fault, but we are part of the society that tolerates them. Should we not, like Ezra, pour out our hearts in shame for the evils in our land, and particularly for the failure of the Church to act as salt and light? Instead, we often allow our attitudes to be shaped by society which has no loyalty to God.

Thought for the day

Christ calls us to be like salt among rotting meat and light in a dark place.

Prayer for the day

Lord, I am ashamed that I get inured to the evil in society and in myself. Please help me to live a wholesome and distinctive life that brings credit to you.

MG

11

Nehemiah: an arrow prayer

In the month of Nisan, in the twentieth year of King
Artaxerxes, when wine was served to him, I carried the
wine and gave it to the king. Now, I had never been sad
in his presence before. So the king said to me, 'Why is
your face sad, since you are not sick? This can only be
sadness of the heart.' Then I was very much afraid. I said
to the king, 'May the king live for ever! Why should my
face not be sad, when the city, the place of my ancestors'
graves, lies waste, and its gates have been destroyed by
fire?' Then the king said to me, 'What do you request?'
So I prayed to the God of heaven. Then I said to the
king, 'If it pleases the king, and if your servant has found
favour with you, I ask that you send me to Judah, to the
city of my ancestors' graves, so that I may rebuild it.' The
king said to me (the queen also was sitting beside him),
'How long will you be gone, and when will you return?'
So it pleased the king to send me, and I set him a date.
Then I said to the king, 'If it pleases the king, let letters
be given me to the governors of the province Beyond
the River, that they may grant me passage until I arrive
in Judah; and a letter to Asaph, the keeper of the king's

forest, directing him to give me timber to make beams for the gates of the temple fortress, and for the wall of the city, and for the house that I shall occupy.' And the king granted me what I asked, for the gracious hand of my God was upon me.

Then I came to the governors of the province Beyond the River, and gave them the king's letters.

(Nehemiah 2.1–9)

Ezra and Nehemiah (one book in the Hebrew Bible) are concerned with the greatest highlight in Judaism after the exodus, the return from exile in Babylon. Ezra supervises the more religious reforms, to which Nehemiah provides a social and political counterpart. This first-hand record by Nehemiah takes us to 446 BC, some 12 years after Ezra and his contingent returned to Jerusalem. There are some difficulties in the chronology (there were three kings called Artaxerxes!), but it is clear that local tribes were fiercely opposed to the return of the exiles and success-fully petitioned the Persian king to prevent a defensive wall being built round Jerusalem (see Ezra 4).

Nehemiah was a Jew who had not returned to Jerusalem but occupied an important position as cupbearer to the Persian king. The cupbearer had to taste the wine before the king drank, in case it was poisoned. Chapter 1 tells of his deep distress at hearing that morale among the returned exiles was low, with the walls of the city remaining broken down and its gates burnt with fire – presumably ever since Nebuchadnezzar's sack of the city in 587 BC.

The first thing Nehemiah does after hearing the news is to pray (1.4–11). Drawing on the rich liturgical prayers of his people, he bows in awe and wonder before the God of heaven. He then turns to confession of both personal and national sin. Only after this does he claim God's covenant love for the people, and prays for an opportunity to raise the matter with the king – a delicate matter since a previous king had forbidden the wall to be rebuilt.

Nehemiah has much to teach us about prayer. As soon as he heard bad news he turned to prayer, serious prayer with adoration, confession and fasting. He prayed like this for four months (1.1; 2.1), and one day, when on duty, he could not hide his sorrow. This could have led to his execution – you were meant to be cheerful, not sorrowful, before the king. But in the providence of God it did not. The king asked him why he was sad, and what request he wanted to make. Then we read a most significant sentence which is a magnificent example to us: 'I prayed to the God of heaven. Then I answered the king . . .' (verse 4). Before he tried to grasp this unforeseen opportunity to go and rectify the situation in Jerusalem, he shot up an 'arrow' prayer to the God of heaven. It must have been very short because he could not delay his answer to the king, but how important it is to make those short prayers in the midst of a busy life. Nehemiah was very much a man of action, yet this book shows how much he prayed (1.4; 4.4, 9; 5.19; 6.9, 14; 13.14, 22, 29, 31). Most of these prayers are very short. Let's learn from Nehemiah, this busy leader, to complement our regular times of prayer with these short arrow prayers in the midst of all our activity. Then, like Nehemiah, we may well find God guiding us through circumstances.

Thought for the day

Short prayers can open big doors.

Prayer for the day

Lord, help me to lift my heart to you in brief prayer at odd moments of the day.

MG

12

Job: God makes no mistakes

Then Job answered the LORD:

'I know that you can do all things,
   and that no purpose of yours can be thwarted.
"Who is this that hides counsel without knowledge?"
Therefore I have uttered what I did not understand,
   things too wonderful for me, which I did not know.
"Hear, and I will speak;
   I will question you, and you declare to me."
I had heard of you by the hearing of the ear,
   but now my eye sees you;
therefore I despise myself,
   and repent in dust and ashes.'

(Job 42.1–6)

I find much of the book of Job quite confusing. It is hard to discern between truth and half-truth in the long speeches where the God-fearing Job and his friends discuss the cause of his intense suffering and how he should react. But while many of their words express truth, their attitudes distort their conclusions – Job in his self-justification, his friends in their smug condemnation of his self-righteousness. At last the three friends give up; Job is clearly not listening to their proffered 'wisdom'. A younger man, Elihu, silent till now, steps in (with an even longer speech!), angry with Job for his self-justification and with the three others for their failure to help and for their condemnation of their supposed friend. Job, he says, stop blaming God for your troubles and for what seems to you to be his unjust treatment. 'Of a truth, God will not do wickedly, and the Almighty will not pervert justice' (34.12). Stop and listen to God. 'Hear this, O Job; stop and consider the wondrous works of God' (37.14).

At last Job is ready to listen, and the Lord speaks to him. 'Where were you when I laid the foundation of the earth?' (38.4). God points him to many aspects of Creation and shows Job his power and wisdom. So we come to today's verses. Job is humbled. He acknowledges the Lord's sovereignty and wisdom, confesses his own impoverished understanding and repents deeply of his pride. I like verse 5, when in effect Job says, 'I knew about you before, but now I really know you.'

In 42.2 he says, 'I know that you can do all things and no purpose of yours can be thwarted.' I first read these words at a time of pain and confusion in my own life. I had speed-read the book, thinking it would have something to say to me, but was still confused. Until I came to these words. It was one of those times (rare for me) when it seemed that God himself took his highlighting pen. He showed me his sovereignty. He showed me that he is a God who never, ever, makes a mistake. I saw that there is no point in trusting a God who might be right just 98 per cent of the time; he had to be right 100 per cent (even 110 per cent!). To change the image, it seemed that he held an outsize mallet and he hammered a strong post deep into the ground beside me, over a metre tall, with the diameter of a telegraph pole. That post was completely solid, unmoveable. It showed me that he is utterly reliable and reminded me of Moses' words in Deuteronomy 32.4:

> The Rock, his work is perfect,
> and all his ways are just.
> A faithful God, without deceit,
> just and upright is he.

I hang on to that secure post of God's unfailing wisdom and his long-term perspective (with the long-distance, sharp eyesight of a high-flying eagle, unlike my worm's-eye view) when I look at the world and wonder why he allows so much war and injustice. And I hang on to it when things in my own life seem insecure. Not long ago, wet macular degeneration (MD) in my right eye was not detected early enough, so some permanent damage has left a blind spot in my central vision. Now wet MD has been diagnosed in my left eye – my supposed 'good' eye. Hopefully injections will stay the trouble, but there are plenty of uncertainties. What will this mean to my lifestyle? To independence? To driving? To reading, using the computer, cooking, knitting? Even, 'What if I go blind?' Those are some of the questions, the fears. But God *is* sovereign. He is in control. He knows the future, he makes no mistakes; Job helps me to trust him.

Thought for the day

God doesn't get things wrong, even when we think he has.

Prayer for the day

Thank you, Lord, that you really are 100 per cent trustworthy.

RG

13

A psalmist: a victorious God

Why do the nations conspire,
  and the peoples plot in vain?
The kings of the earth set themselves,
  and the rulers take counsel together,
  against the LORD and his anointed, saying,
'Let us burst their bonds asunder,
  and cast their cords from us.'

He who sits in the heavens laughs;
  the LORD has them in derision.
Then he will speak to them in his wrath,
  and terrify them in his fury, saying,
'I have set my king on Zion, my holy hill.'

I will tell of the decree of the LORD:
He said to me, 'You are my son;
  today I have begotten you.
Ask of me, and I will make the nations your heritage,
  and the ends of the earth your possession.
You shall break them with a rod of iron,
  and dash them in pieces like a potter's vessel.'

Now therefore, O kings, be wise;

    be warned, O rulers of the earth.

Serve the LORD with fear,

    with trembling kiss his feet,

.or he will be angry, and you will perish in the way;

    for his wrath is quickly kindled.

Happy are all who take refuge in him.

(Psalm 2)

Let's take a peek at a scene a good many centuries after this psalm was written. It is probably AD 30. A group of Christians is gathered in the Upper Room. Peter and John come in, fresh from their encounter with the Sanhedrin, the religious council of the high priest and other Jewish leaders. They have been reprimanded for Peter's bold preaching about Jesus and his resurrection. A crowd had gathered after the remarkable healing, in the Temple precincts, of a 40-year-old man who had been crippled from birth. Peter and John were utterly fearless in their declaration of Jesus as the only Saviour (Acts 4.12) and their refusal to obey the Sanhedrin's injunction to stay silent (4.19, 20). Reporting back to their friends, they don't hold an alarmed discussion about what they should do. They all turn straight to prayer to the Creator God, and then quote from Psalm 2. I guess that one of the group starts the psalm and the rest (who know their

Scriptures!) join in the whole psalm, not just the verses Luke quotes in Acts. 'He who sits in the heavens laughs . . . I have set my king on Zion, my holy hill.' God is victorious. The disciples are confident of that, despite their current predicament. The psalmist rejoiced, though of course he could not know how those future disciples would need the assurance of his words.

The psalmist did not understand fully what he was writing. Nevertheless, as he continued he again looked forward to the future. 'He [the Lord] said to me, "You are my son; today I have begotten you."' The writer of the psalm may have thought that was just a special promise from the Lord to him. But St Paul saw it otherwise. Preaching in Pisidian Antioch, Roman colony in central Turkey, he told his hearers, 'We bring you the good news that what God promised to our ancestors he has fulfilled for us, their children, by raising Jesus: as also it is written in the second psalm, "You are my Son . . ."' (Acts 13.32–33). The writer of the epistle to the Hebrews echoes the same verse in Hebrews 1.1–2 as he affirms the superiority of Jesus over the angels: 'Long ago God spoke to our ancestors . . . by the prophets, but in these last days he has spoken to us by a Son.' We have the privilege of God's perspective that the writer of the psalm didn't have – a privilege we should not take for granted.

Read the psalm again and think of the perspective the

psalmist had – and those early Christians – and ourselves. Verse 8 says, 'I will make the nations your heritage, and the ends of the earth your possession.' That is the right of the One who will come in glory at the second Advent. As we look at the world today, so much of it in a mess, we can pray for that fulfilment of God's glory to come; and each of us can ask the Lord what part he wants us to play in seeking to bring his kingdom on earth (as we pray regularly in the Lord's Prayer) through our intentional prayer, through our actions, through our words.

Thought for the day

The Lord is supreme so we can pray to him confidently, whatever mess we see on earth.

Prayer for the day

'Your kingdom come, your will be done on earth as it is in heaven.' Lord, please show me what small part you want me to play to see that prayer fulfilled.

RG

14

A psalmist: desolation

My God, my God, why have you forsaken me?
  Why are you so far from helping me, from the words
  of my groaning?
O my God, I cry by day, but you do not answer;
  and by night, but find no rest.

Yet you are holy,
  enthroned on the praises of Israel.
In you our ancestors trusted;
  they trusted, and you delivered them.
To you they cried, and were saved;
  in you they trusted, and were not put to shame.

But I am a worm, and not human;
  scorned by others, and despised by the people.
All who see me mock at me;
  they make mouths at me, they shake their heads;
'Commit your cause to the LORD; let him deliver –
  let him rescue the one in whom he delights!'

Yet it was you who took me from the womb;
  you kept me safe on my mother's breast.
On you I was cast from my birth,

and since my mother bore me you have been my God.
Do not be far from me,
    for trouble is near
    and there is no one to help.

Many bulls encircle me,
    strong bulls of Bashan surround me;
they open wide their mouths at me,
    like a ravening and roaring lion.

I am poured out like water,
    and all my bones are out of joint;
my heart is like wax;
    it is melted within my breast;
my mouth is dried up like a potsherd,
    and my tongue sticks to my jaws;
    you lay me in the dust of death.

For dogs are all around me;
    a company of evildoers encircles me.
My hands and feet have shrivelled;
I can count all my bones.
They stare and gloat over me;
they divide my clothes among themselves,
    and for my clothing they cast lots.

But you, O Lord, do not be far away!
    O my help, come quickly to my aid!
Deliver my soul from the sword,

my life from the power of the dog!
Save me from the mouth of the lion!

From the horns of the wild oxen you have rescued me.
I will tell of your name to my brothers and sisters;
    in the midst of the congregation I will praise you:
You who fear the LORD, praise him!
    All you offspring of Jacob, glorify him;
    stand in awe of him, all you offspring of Israel!
For he did not despise or abhor
    the affliction of the afflicted;
he did not hide his face from me,
    but heard when I cried to him.

From you comes my praise in the great congregation;
    my vows I will pay before those who fear him.
The poor shall eat and be satisfied;
    those who seek him shall praise the LORD.
    May your hearts live for ever!

All the ends of the earth shall remember
    and turn to the LORD;
and all the families of the nations
    shall worship before him.
For dominion belongs to the LORD,
    and he rules over the nations.

To him, indeed, shall all who sleep in the earth bow
    down;

before him shall bow all who go down to the dust,
and I shall live for him.
Posterity will serve him;

future generations will be told about the Lord,
and proclaim his deliverance to a people yet unborn,
saying that he has done it.

(Psalm 22)

'My God, my God, why have you forsaken me?' We hear Jesus' despairing cry from the cross, but before we think about that scene, let's think first about David. We do not know what his situation was when he wrote this psalm. Was it when his first son, born out of wedlock, was desperately ill? Was it when King Saul and his armies were pursuing him? Or when his rebellious son Absalom had been killed? David was in agony, feeling that the God whom he loved and trusted had deserted him. God's silence was even worse than the pain of the situation. 'I cry by day, but you do not answer; and by night, but find no rest.'

'*Yet* you are holy, enthroned on the praises of Israel.' He affirmed God as mighty. He knew his forefathers had trusted him and been rescued by him. He himself had trusted God since he was young. In the midst of fearsome attack (verses 12–18) he prayed for rescue – no longer in total despair, but trusting God to answer (verses 19–21) and calling others to join him in praise (verses 22, 23). His Lord has heard him.

So we think again of Jesus and his cry from the cross. For David, the greatest pain was to feel that God had deserted him. For Jesus, that sense of desertion was even worse. His communication with his heavenly Father had always been close. Now, on the cross, the sin of the world separated him from the Holy One who, we are told, 'cannot look on wrongdoing' (Habakkuk 1.13). I like the illustration of this that can be demonstrated using two upturned hands. One hand represents Jesus, with nothing between him and the light above. The other hand, weighed down by a black bag, represents us, in the shadow, separated from God by our sin. Isaiah wrote, 'The LORD has laid on him the iniquity of us all' (Isaiah 53.6). So the weight is transferred from the 'me' hand to the 'Jesus' hand. I am no longer separated from God; I am free to communicate with him. But Jesus called out, 'My God, why have you forsaken me?' in his agony of being cut off from his Father.

There are many verses in this psalm that were fulfilled in Jesus' death. The 'bulls' who surrounded him, who stared at him, gloated over him; the mocking of those who said, 'He trusts in God; let God deliver him now'; his thirst; his hands and feet pierced in crucifixion; his clothing divided up by casting lots. We might almost think that those who crucified him were trying to fulfil the prophecies of the psalm! But Jesus knew that psalm.

He knew how it progressed from pain to praise. Even as he called out he knew there was victory ahead, as there was for David, because he knew his purpose in coming to this world, that he came to 'give his life as a ransom for many'.

What a mighty encouragement for us when we are in pain – and our suffering can never be as deep as it was for Jesus. I remember thinking, at a time of great difficulty in my life, that however deep and dark a well I might feel I was in, Jesus had been in a deeper, darker place. He was always there, with his promise, 'I will never leave you or forsake you.' Jesus was brought through to the resurrection. The psalmist was sustained and brought through to praise. And he will bring me as well through to victory.

Thought for the day

We have a God who is with us in the very darkest places, even when we cannot feel his presence.

Prayer for the day

Lord, please help me to claim the promise that you never, never desert us.

RG

15

A psalmist: King of Glory

The earth is the Lord's and all that is in it,
　　the world, and those who live in it;
for he has founded it on the seas,
　　and established it on the rivers.

Who shall ascend the hill of the Lord?
　　And who shall stand in his holy place?
Those who have clean hands and pure hearts,
　　who do not lift up their souls to what is false,
　　and do not swear deceitfully.
They will receive blessing from the Lord,
　　and vindication from the God of their salvation.
Such is the company of those who seek him,
　　who seek the face of the God of Jacob.

Lift up your heads, O gates!
　　and be lifted up, O ancient doors!
　　that the King of glory may come in.
Who is the King of glory?
　　The Lord, strong and mighty,
　　the Lord, mighty in battle.
Lift up your heads, O gates!

and be lifted up, O ancient doors!

that the King of glory may come in.

Who is this King of glory?

The LORD of hosts,

he is the King of glory.

(Psalm 24)

'The earth is the LORD's', David proclaims confidently. Sadly there are many in our own nation who deny that and have no intention of admitting that they live in his world or are subject to him. 'But that's not true of me,' you say to yourself; 'I'm all right!'

I, too, am sure he is Creator of the universe – including me. But David faces each of us with a challenge, as he sets a high standard for those who seek to 'ascend the hill of the LORD' to enter his presence. Clean hands; a pure heart; purity in behaviour, thought and speech, that we may be people of integrity and truth. However hard we strive, we cannot do it by ourselves. We can enter his presence only as people forgiven through Jesus' suffering on the cross, who have his living Spirit to change us from within. Read verses 3–6 again in the light of New Testament experience.

In verse 7, David moves from seeking the face of the God of Jacob, from climbing to 'ascend the hill of the LORD', to his coming in glory. Despite prophecies of a suffering, servant Messiah, the Jews expected him to come as king over all. We move from thinking of the first

Advent, Jesus born on earth in humility, to the second Advent, when he will return again. When I grew up the main focus of the Advent season was his return at the Second Coming. Nowadays the prospect of his return is almost forgotten and the focus of Advent is mostly on preparations for our Christmas celebrations, both spiritual and material. 'Lift up your heads . . . that the King of glory may come in!' says David. And Jesus speaks of the day when he will come again: 'They will see the Son of Man coming on the clouds of heaven with power and great glory' (Matthew 24.30). We don't know exactly what it will be like – the New Testament paints various pictures – but it will be glorious and unmistakable. We don't know when it will be, but it will be sudden and unexpected. In the same chapter Jesus warns us to be ready at any time, for no one – not even the angels, not even the Son – knows when that time will be.

The ageing John wrote of Jesus' return, 'When he is revealed, we will be like him, for we will see him as he is' (1 John 3.2). That is amazing. 'We will be like him', reflecting his brightness and his glory. John continues, 'All who have this hope in him purify themselves, just as he is pure.' The thought of his return is a stimulus to how I live now. I do not want to be ashamed when he returns (as I am ashamed when my husband appears unexpectedly and finds me playing a computer card game – again! That is a micro part of the shame I will feel when Jesus returns if I am engaged in something I know he wouldn't like). So we come back to David's standard of purity. Verse 4 covers our actions, our thoughts, our attitudes, our speech; that is pretty comprehensive. If I live like that, I will not need to be ashamed when the King of Glory returns in all his splendour.

Thought for the day

Jesus will come again, not in humble obscurity but as King of all Creation.

Prayer for the day

Lord, please help to be ready for your return, whenever that may be.

RG

16

A psalmist: a God who forgives

Have mercy on me, O God,
   according to your steadfast love;
according to your abundant mercy
   blot out my transgressions.
Wash me thoroughly from my iniquity,
   and cleanse me from my sin.

For I know my transgressions,
   and my sin is ever before me.
Against you, you alone, have I sinned,
   and done what is evil in your sight,
so that you are justified in your sentence
   and blameless when you pass judgement.
Indeed, I was born guilty,
   a sinner when my mother conceived me.

You desire truth in the inward being;
   therefore teach me wisdom in my secret heart.
Purge me with hyssop, and I shall be clean;
   wash me, and I shall be whiter than snow.
Let me hear joy and gladness;
   let the bones that you have crushed rejoice.

Hide your face from my sins,
    and blot out all my iniquities.

Create in me a clean heart, O God,
    and put a new and right spirit within me.
Do not cast me away from your presence,
    and do not take your holy spirit from me.
Restore to me the joy of your salvation,
    and sustain in me a willing spirit.

Then I will teach transgressors your ways,
    and sinners will return to you.
Deliver me from bloodshed, O God,
    O God of my salvation,
    and my tongue will sing aloud of your deliverance.

O Lord, open my lips,
    and my mouth will declare your praise.
For you have no delight in sacrifice;
    if I were to give a burnt-offering, you would not be
    pleased.
The sacrifice acceptable to God is a broken spirit;
    a broken and contrite heart, O God, you will not despise.
Do good to Zion in your good pleasure;
    rebuild the walls of Jerusalem,
then you will delight in right sacrifices,
    in burnt-offerings and whole burnt-offerings;
    then bulls will be offered on your altar.

(Psalm 51)

'I know that God forgives me, but I cannot forgive myself.' How often have I heard that comment from a person struggling with feelings of guilt (whether real or false guilt). I often reply, 'If a holy God forgives you, what right do you have to hold on to your own guilt feelings?' This is a psalm for guilt-ridden Christians who say, 'Yes, I know God forgives. But can he really forgive me for . . .' and out comes an admission of guilt or shame. David was indeed guilty. We read the shameful story of progressive sin in 2 Samuel chapter 11. David's lust led to adultery with another man's wife, Bathsheba. When he learnt that she was pregnant, he called her husband Uriah back from battle to entice him into sleeping with her, so the baby could be passed off as his. Attempted deceit. That didn't work, despite getting Uriah drunk. So David sent orders to the commander-in-chief for Uriah to be sent into the front line to ensure he was killed. Indirect murder. What a sad tale for a God-fearing king!

But David couldn't get away with his sin for ever. Nathan the prophet was courageous enough to confront the king, leading to David's clear confession: 'I have sinned against the LORD' (2 Samuel 12.13). Psalm 51 is his prayer of confession and repentance, and shows the freedom that comes from the assurance of being forgiven. David first throws himself on God's compassion and mercy. He knows he doesn't deserve to be forgiven, he knows that God's judgement on him is justified: transgression, sin, iniquity, evil are the words he uses of himself, for he acknowledges not only his sinful behaviour but even his sinful nature, tainted from birth. ('Original sin' is the phrase we use. What parent can deny this? No infant is taught to disobey; it comes naturally!)

So he asks for his sin to be blotted out. Isaiah declared, from God, 'I am He who blots out your transgressions for my own sake, and I will not remember your sins' (Isaiah 43.25). That is the verse a friend showed me when I felt deeply guilty at the way I had just treated my mother-in-law; I needed to know, as never before, that God would forgive me. He blots out our transgression. Blots it out. Eradicates it. It is as if he presses the Delete button on his computer – not the Undo button. It has gone. In old-fashioned terminology, the slate is wiped clean. Why? 'For my own sake.' Not just because he loves us, but to satisfy his own character of holiness and love. What is more, he does not remember. He forgets the sin was ever committed. That is utterly amazing. And he wants us to grasp it, not just in our heads but in our inner being. That may be a slow process, and we may have to repeat the prayer – like the saucepans I often burn, that need more than one soaking and scrubbing to get them really clean.

David prayed, too, 'Wash me, and I shall be whiter than snow.' Isaiah again: 'Though your sins are like scarlet,

72

they shall be like snow' (Isaiah 1.18). The scarlet dye they used was unbleachable, yet the Lord bleaches the scarlet sin, to be as white as newly fallen snow. So David asks to be cleansed through and through. This is no shallow confession; there is a sense of deep penitence. And the rest of the psalm shows that he did indeed grasp that he was truly forgiven. He expects to lead other sinners to repentance (verse 33). He prays for the joy of his salvation to be restored and then erupts in praise.

Thought for the day

David, like many other people, deserved judgement but received forgiveness.

Prayer for the day

Thank you, Lord, that I can experience you really forgiving me and I can rejoice in your freedom.

RG

17

A psalmist: God lifts me up

Save me, O God,
    for the waters have come up to my neck.
I sink in deep mire,
    where there is no foothold;
I have come into deep waters,
    and the flood sweeps over me.
I am weary with my crying;
    my throat is parched.
My eyes grow dim
    with waiting for my God.

More in number than the hairs of my head
    are those who hate me without cause;
many are those who would destroy me,
    my enemies who accuse me falsely.
What I did not steal
    must I now restore?
O God, you know my folly;
    the wrongs I have done are not hidden from you.

Do not let those who hope in you be put to shame
    because of me,

O Lord GOD of hosts;
do not let those who seek you be dishonoured because
    of me,
    O God of Israel.
It is for your sake that I have borne reproach,
    that shame has covered my face.
I have become a stranger to my kindred,
    an alien to my mother's children.

It is zeal for your house that has consumed me;
    the insults of those who insult you have fallen on me.
When I humbled my soul with fasting,
    they insulted me for doing so.
When I made sackcloth my clothing,
    I became a byword to them.
I am the subject of gossip for those who sit in the gate,
    and the drunkards make songs about me.

But as for me, my prayer is to you, O LORD.
    At an acceptable time, O God,
    in the abundance of your steadfast love, answer me.
With your faithful help rescue me
    from sinking in the mire;
let me be delivered from my enemies
    and from the deep waters.
Do not let the flood sweep over me,
    or the deep swallow me up,
    or the Pit close its mouth over me.

Answer me, O Lord, for your steadfast love is good;
 according to your abundant mercy, turn to me.
Do not hide your face from your servant,
 for I am in distress – make haste to answer me.
Draw near to me, redeem me,
 set me free because of my enemies.

You know the insults I receive,
 and my shame and dishonour;
 my foes are all known to you.
Insults have broken my heart,
 so that I am in despair.
I looked for pity, but there was none;
 and for comforters, but I found none.
They gave me poison for food,
 and for my thirst they gave me vinegar to drink.

(Psalm 69.1–21)

I remember a day, decades ago, when I was feeling utterly dejected. A friend, wanting to encourage me, turned to this psalm and started to read at verse 13. 'My prayer is to you, O Lord . . . With your faithful help rescue me from sinking in the mire.' But in my depression I wasn't ready for that! I insisted that she read from the beginning of the psalm. 'The waters have come up to my neck . . . I sink in deep mire . . . the flood sweeps over me.' That was where my feelings were. I needed to know that the psalmist (whose situation was probably even worse than mine) identified with me in my misery before I was ready to join him in his prayer of verses 16–18: 'Answer me, O LORD, for your steadfast love is good; according to your abundant mercy turn to me. Do not hide your face from your servant . . . Draw near to me, redeem me, set me free.'

There are many psalms that start dismally but end in praise. We can often see a clear moment when the psalmist chooses to change direction, to look up rather than down. It is the same in chapter 3 of Lamentations, 20 verses that are the most woeful of all Jeremiah's woes, with one image after another to describe how shut off from God he feels. Then comes the turning point in verse 21: 'But this I call to mind, and therefore I have hope. The steadfast love of the Lord never ceases, his mercies never come to an end.' We do not necessarily burst through immediately into 100 per cent praise, but the choice has been made; we refuse to wallow in the mud for ever. I see it like standing in the centre of a see-saw: a slight change of weight one way or the other decides which end goes up, which down. I can say, 'I know God is good but my life is miserable' – and I stay stuck in the negative. Or I can say, 'My life is miserable but I know God is good' – and I shift into a positive attitude. In the following verses the psalmist still expresses his pain, but with a more positive note; he expects God to help. We do not ignore our pain, but we invite his Spirit into it, to share it and heal it.

What are we to make of the psalmist's diatribe against his enemies and his request for God to judge them? As a Christian I cannot join in the apparent desire for revenge. But in this psalm, as in many others, I think not of human enemies but of the enemy of souls; then I can enter vehemently in prayer against the one of whom Jesus warned, 'Fear him who, after he has killed, has power to cast into hell' (Luke 12.5). We have a spiritual enemy who is indeed powerful – but less powerful than the King of kings.

So I was encouraged that day with my friend, as I found the psalmist identifying with me in my depression. Another excitement came later. One morning the reading in church was John's account of Jesus turning the money-changers out of the Temple. In John 2.17, 'His disciples remembered that it was written, "Zeal for your house will consume me."' I looked inquisitively for the cross-reference, and found it in Psalm 69.9. So the psalm wasn't only about the psalmist and me; it was also about the Messiah. Wow! I looked further. 'I have become a stranger to my kindred, an alien to my mother's children' (verse 8). In his lifetime Jesus' brothers disowned him. 'For my thirst they gave me vinegar to drink' (verse 21) on the cross. It was not only the psalmist who understood my depression, but Jesus – not just the divine Jesus with his X-ray eyes, but the Jesus who lived on earth and experienced human joys and sorrows. I can imagine Jesus on the cross praying much of this psalm – but with verses 22–28 replaced by his prayer of forgiveness towards his persecutors.

Thought for the day

However depressed and isolated I may feel, I am never alone. Jesus, in his humanity, is alongside.

Prayer for the day

Thank you, Jesus, that you identify with me in all my sorrows and my joys.

RG

18

Isaiah: we worship a holy, forgiving God

In the year that King Uzziah died, I saw the Lord sitting on a throne, high and lofty; and the hem of his robe filled the temple. Seraphs were in attendance above him; each had six wings: with two they covered their faces, and with two they covered their feet, and with two they flew. And one called to another and said:

> 'Holy, holy, holy is the LORD of hosts;
> the whole earth is full of his glory.'

The pivots on the thresholds shook at the voices of those who called, and the house filled with smoke. And I said: 'Woe is me! I am lost, for I am a man of unclean lips, and I live among a people of unclean lips; yet my eyes have seen the King, the LORD of hosts!'

Then one of the seraphs flew to me, holding a live coal that had been taken from the altar with a pair of tongs. The seraph touched my mouth with it and said: 'Now that this has touched your lips, your guilt has departed and your sin is blotted out.' Then I heard the voice of the Lord

saying, 'Whom shall I send, and who will go for us?' And
I said, 'Here am I; send me!' (Isaiah 6.1–8)

'In the year that King Uzziah died . . .' I like the way that
Isaiah clearly roots his sacred experience of God in history,
in 740 or 739 BC. In the very first verse of his book he says
that he received his prophetic message during the reign of
four kings, spanning about 40 years. He must have been
quite a young man when he had this clear vision of the
Lord. I guess he was in total awe as he wrote of God seated
on his throne, his garment spread out, filling the temple.
That says something of the hugeness of the image. The
angels flew round him in worship, their faces covered, in
awe at the Lord's presence. Their worship proclaimed his
holiness, as did the four 'living creatures' in John's vision
of heaven in Revelation chapter 4. They sang, 'Holy, holy,
holy, the Lord God the Almighty, who was and is and is
to come.' Others joined in, 'You are worthy, our Lord and
God, to receive glory and honour and power.' We can use
these songs of worship to express our own worship to this
almighty, holy God. Many of our prayers – our thanks, our
confession, our intercession – are concerned with God in
relation to our lives on earth. Worship is concerned with
God and who he is. I love the story of the small boy who,
in a fit of temper, smashed his favourite toy on the floor.
When Daddy returned home, the boy's words were, 'Sorry

I got cross; please will you mend it?' and – the job finished – 'Thank you, Daddy.' And as he watched the repair being made, he exclaimed, 'Daddy, aren't you wonderful!' Our worship says to God, 'Aren't you wonderful!'

Isaiah was overawed by the realization of God's holiness and majesty; it left him very aware of his own unworthiness before such a God. However 'good' or 'bad' we are, we are grubby beside the utter purity of a holy God. But, amazingly, that holy God loves his spoilt, fallen creatures. He had a purpose for Isaiah, so it was divine initiative that sent the angel with fire to touch his lips and burn away the 'uncleanness' of which Isaiah was so conscious. And it was divine, loving initiative that sent Jesus to live and die for us.

What a wonderful promise Isaiah heard from the angel! 'Your guilt has departed and your sin is blotted out' (verse 8). Often we know in our heads that God forgives us, but we still hear an inner voice whispering, 'Surely I can't be forgiven for this particular wrong; I don't deserve it.' No, I don't deserve it, but he still holds out his forgiveness, which I can choose to accept or spurn. I find it a help to turn familiar words from 1 John 1.9 into a personal prayer: 'If I confess my sins, you who are faithful and just will forgive my sins and cleanse me from all unrighteousness. Thank you, Lord.' I may need to repeat that prayer many times, to let its truth seep into the core of my being. If the doctor prescribes a course of antibiotics, I don't take just one pill and say, 'I'm not better yet; the pills can't be any good.' I need to take the whole course. Yes, a holy God, who 'ought' to punish me or exclude me entirely, loves me enough to forgive me, to count me clean, because of Jesus.

But the Lord hadn't finished with Isaiah. He had a job for him to do – not a command but an invitation. 'Whom shall I send, and who will go for us?' The forgiven Isaiah was ready to offer himself for service, even without a specific job description: 'Lord, send me.' May that be my prayer, and yours, today.

Thought for the day

How amazing that an utterly pure, holy God should want to forgive his unholy children.

Prayer for the day

Lord, please help me to worship and serve you in the confidence that you forgive me.

RG

19

Jeremiah: God's presence in weakness

Now the word of the LORD came to me saying,

> 'Before I formed you in the womb I knew you,
> and before you were born I consecrated you;
> I appointed you a prophet to the nations.'

Then I said, 'Ah, Lord GOD! Truly I do not know how to speak, for I am only a boy.' But the LORD said to me,

> 'Do not say, "I am only a boy";
> for you shall go to all to whom I send you,
> and you shall speak whatever I command you.
> Do not be afraid of them,
> for I am with you to deliver you,
> says the LORD.'

Then the LORD put out his hand and touched my mouth; and the LORD said to me,

> 'Now I have put my words in your mouth.
> See, today I appoint you over nations and over
>   kingdoms,
> to pluck up and to pull down,

to destroy and to overthrow,
to build and to plant.'

(Jeremiah 1.4–10)

How would you feel if you had a strong conviction that
you were called to a certain course of action but knew
from the outset it was doomed to failure? That was the
fate of Jeremiah. Born of a priestly family in the last fateful
years of the kingdom of Judah before it was swept off into
Babylonian captivity, he may well have expected a quiet
religious life. No such luck! God broke into his life when
he was still a young man and called him to an extremely
difficult task – to warn Judah of her fate, to explain that
it was due to her apostasy, and to be personally involved
in the debacle, since he was carried off to Egypt by some
refugees from Nebuchadnezzar's capture of Jerusalem in
587 BC. Jeremiah was a sensitive man, which must have
made it worse. Indeed, at times he felt it was all too much
and wished he had never been born (see his desperate
prayer in 20.7–end) but, on the whole, he carried out his
calling with distinction over 40 years.

Overwhelmed by the call to be a prophet, his response
was predictable: 'Ah, Lord GOD! Truly I do not know how
to speak, for I am only a boy' (verse 6). He was actually a
young man of about 20, but he felt utterly dwarfed by the
prospect, particularly as it was primarily to 'to pluck up

and to pull down, to destroy and to overthrow' (verse 10), although Jeremiah was also to be the prophet of return after exile, hence his call 'to build and to plant' (verse 10). More than that, he would predict the new covenant to be written on the heart of the believer (31.27–40). He even had an inkling of Jesus as the righteous Branch through whom Israel would be saved (23.5ff).

Three things seem to have sustained him for this job he did not want to do. One was the thought that God knew him intimately, had formed him in the womb and had chosen him for this difficult task (verse 5).

The second was that God promised to put his words in Jeremiah's mouth so that it would not be a mere man denouncing Judah in its decline, but the word of the Lord (verse 9).

The third thing that must have meant so much to him was the promise: '"I am with you to deliver you," says the LORD' (verse 8). This did not mean he would not have to undergo scorn, suffering, imprisonment and exile. He would. But in all these things God would stay with him and sustain him (verses 9, 19).

Jeremiah's situation is so very different from ours, but if we feel called to some action that we fear is going to be extremely difficult, we too can rest on the fact that God knows us through and through and has called us to it. We too can expect him to equip us for the task, however inadequate we feel, and be confident of his promise, 'I am with you always, to the end of the age' (Matthew 28.20).

Thought for the day

'Before I formed you in the womb I knew you . . . and set you apart' (verse 5).

Prayer for the day

Lord, when I feel events are overwhelming me, help me to remember that you know me intimately, you sustain me and you will never forsake me.

MG

20

Daniel: committed to pray

The men said, 'We shall not find any ground for complaint against this Daniel unless we find it in connection with the law of his God.'

So the presidents and satraps conspired and came to the king and said to him, 'O King Darius, live for ever! All the presidents of the kingdom, the prefects and the satraps, the counsellors and the governors, are agreed that the king should establish an ordinance and enforce an interdict, that whoever prays to anyone, divine or human, for thirty days, except to you, O king, shall be thrown into a den of lions. Now, O king, establish the interdict and sign the document, so that it cannot be changed, according to the law of the Medes and the Persians, which cannot be revoked.' Therefore King Darius signed the document and interdict.

Although Daniel knew that the document had been signed, he continued to go to his house, which had windows in its upper room open towards Jerusalem, and to get down on his knees three times a day to pray to his God and praise him, just as he had done previously. The conspirators came and found Daniel praying and seeking mercy before his God. Then they approached the king and said concerning the interdict, 'O king! Did you not sign an interdict, that anyone who prays to anyone, divine or human, within thirty days except to you, O king, shall be thrown into a den of lions?' The king answered, 'The thing stands fast, according to the law of the Medes and Persians, which cannot be revoked.' Then they responded to the king, 'Daniel, one of the exiles from Judah, pays no attention to you, O king, or to the interdict you have signed, but he is saying his prayers three times a day.'

When the king heard the charge, he was very much distressed. He was determined to save Daniel, and until the sun went down he made every effort to rescue him. Then the conspirators came to the king and said to him, 'Know, O king, that it is a law of the Medes and Persians that no interdict or ordinance that the king establishes can be changed.'

Then the king gave the command, and Daniel was brought and thrown into the den of lions. The king said to Daniel, 'May your God, whom you faithfully serve, deliver you!' A stone was brought and laid on the mouth of the den, and the king sealed it with his own signet and with the signet of his lords, so that nothing might be changed concerning Daniel. Then the king went to his palace and spent the night fasting; no food was brought to him, and sleep fled from him.

Then, at break of day, the king got up and hurried to the den of lions. When he came near the den where Daniel was, he cried out anxiously to Daniel, 'O Daniel, servant of the living God, has your God whom you faithfully serve been able to deliver you from the lions?' Daniel then said to the king, 'O king, live for ever! My God sent his angel and shut the lions' mouths so that they would not hurt me, because I was found blameless before him; and also before you, O king, I have done no wrong.' Then the king was exceedingly glad and commanded that Daniel be taken up out of the den. So Daniel was taken up out of the den, and no kind of harm was found on him, because he had trusted in his God. The king gave a command, and those who had accused Daniel were brought and thrown into the den of lions – they, their children, and their wives. Before they reached the bottom of the den the lions overpowered them and broke all their bones in pieces.

Then King Darius wrote to all peoples and nations of every language throughout the whole world: 'May you have abundant prosperity! I make a decree, that in all my royal dominion people should tremble and fear before the God of Daniel:

For he is the living God,
    enduring for ever.
His kingdom shall never be destroyed,

and his dominion has no end.
He delivers and rescues,
    he works signs and wonders in heaven and on earth;
for he has saved Daniel
    from the power of the lions.'

So this Daniel prospered during the reign of Darius and the reign of Cyrus the Persian.   (Daniel 6.5–28)

Now therefore, O our God, listen to the prayer of your servant and to his supplication, and for your own sake, Lord, let your face shine upon your desolated sanctuary. Incline your ear, O my God, and hear. Open your eyes and look at our desolation and the city that bears your name. We do not present our supplication before you on the ground of our righteousness, but on the ground of your great mercies. O Lord, hear; O Lord, forgive; O Lord, listen and act and do not delay! For your own sake, O my God, because your city and your people bear your name!   (Daniel 9.17–19)

The story of Daniel's deliverance from the den of lions is famous. The story of Daniel the man of prayer is less well known. Yet it was one of the major characteristics of his life (see 2.17, 18; 9.3–19; 10.2–3, 12). Perhaps the most striking feature was its *regularity*. Friends and foes all knew that three times a day Daniel went into an attic room in his house to pray (6.11). Perhaps we feel that we could not commit to regular daily times of prayer because we are too busy. But few of us are as busy as Daniel. He was one of the top three administrators of the Persian empire under Cyrus, whose throne name appears to have been Darius (6.1). Despite being now in his early eighties his work was so exceptional that the king planned to set him over the whole kingdom (6.3). Yet in the midst of all this pressure he made time to pray three times a day. That habit of prayer enhanced his whole life and behaviour. So much so that, in the midst of political intrigue, the only charge against him that his enemies could find was 'in connection with the law of his God' (6.5). They could find 'no grounds for complaint or any corruption, because he was faithful, and no negligence or corruption could be found in him' (6.4). Here was a man in touch with God, and it showed in the way he lived and did his work.

His prayer was *courageous*. When he learnt of the decree that prayer was to be made to no god or man except the king, he went home as usual, opened his attic windows towards Jerusalem and prayed. He knew of course that God is everywhere and hears prayers in Babylon, but Jerusalem was the place where God had supremely made himself known. No doubt he prayed aloud, as the custom was. He could be seen and heard. He knew this could lead to his arrest and execution. Yet he prayed as usual. What courage! He could easily have prayed silently or stayed in his office. But no. He refused to allow even grave danger to interrupt his prayer life.

His prayer was *humble*. While we read of varied prayer postures in the Bible, Daniel got on his knees. He knew that whereas he was great in the kingdom he was small before God. We get a good insight into his humility in the majestic prayer of 9.4–19 where, despite being the most faithful of God's servants, he identifies himself with the sins, disobedience, ingratitude and apostasy of his people. In so doing he points forward to the day when God's righteous Son would take his people's guilt as if it were his own.

Notice the *gratitude* that marked his prayer (6.10) even at such a time of grave personal peril. Finally, we find him asking God for help (6.11). And we know how that prayer was abundantly answered.

But there is one further aspect to his prayer which is uncommon today: his *intensity*. He did not just mention a need, he was passionate in prayer and passionate for God's glory: 'O Lord, hear; O Lord, forgive; O Lord, listen and act and do not delay! For your own sake, O my God, because your city and your people bear your name!' (9.19).

Thought for the day

Regular daily prayer is a must.

Prayer for the day

God, may my life be such that people can blame me only for following you.

MG

21

Jonah: the wideness of God's mercy

Then Jonah prayed to the LORD his God from the belly of
the fish, saying,

'I called to the LORD out of my distress,
   and he answered me;
out of the belly of Sheol I cried,
   and you heard my voice.
You cast me into the deep,
   into the heart of the seas,
   and the flood surrounded me;
all your waves and your billows
   passed over me.
Then I said, 'I am driven away
   from your sight;
how shall I look again
   upon your holy temple?'
The waters closed in over me;
   the deep surrounded me;
weeds were wrapped around my head
   at the roots of the mountains.
I went down to the land
   whose bars closed upon me for ever;

yet you brought up my life from the Pit,
　　O LORD my God.
As my life was ebbing away,
　　I remembered the LORD;
and my prayer came to you,
　　into your holy temple.
Those who worship vain idols
　　forsake their true loyalty.
But I with the voice of thanksgiving
　　will sacrifice to you;
what I have vowed I will pay.
　　Deliverance belongs to the LORD!'

Then the LORD spoke to the fish, and it spewed Jonah out
upon the dry land.   (Jonah 2.1–10)

The book of Jonah is an enigma. Are we meant to take
it literally, as Augustine did? Or more as a parable, as
Origen did? Commentators have been divided ever since.
The literal interpretation is quite possible. Jonah was a real
person, a prophet who lived in the northern kingdom in
the days of Jeroboam II (793–753 BC). He is mentioned
in 2 Kings 14.23–29. There are well-attested cases of men
being swallowed by a whale and surviving. On the other
hand, God's revelation comes not only through history
but through picture, poetry, drama and other literary
genres. Whichever way we take it, it is part of Scripture,

God's revelation to us. And whichever way we take it the message is clear. Israel had lost its vocation to be a light to the Gentiles. It wanted to keep God to itself, and both hated and despised nations like the Assyrians which worshipped other gods. Jonah's resistance to God's call to go to Nineveh and, as the Hebrew may be translated, 'preach to it because its trouble is of concern to me' (1.2) was typical of the attitude of Israel to the surrounding nations.

But that was not God's attitude. His love was not narrowly confined to Israel (nor to churchmen today!) He told Jonah to go to Nineveh, the Assyrian capital, and preach to it. Jonah went – in precisely the opposite direction, no doubt to get away from the territory he thought governed by Yahweh. But Yahweh had a lesson for Jonah. He was no territorial deity but the God of the whole earth, and his compassion reached all his creatures.

Jonah's prayer from inside the great fish is fascinating. It is a thanksgiving psalm such as we find in the psalter. Whether it was his own creation (most prophets were poets as well) or a psalm he had learnt, we do not know. But it is very vivid. The psalm makes it clear that Jonah realized he had been given new life instead of the death he admitted he deserved. He realized that there was no way he could contribute to his rescue: 'Deliverance belongs to the LORD' (verse 9). It is only when he admits this that the great fish vomits him up on dry land. His recognition that God saves whom he will may prefigure the possibility that God would choose to rescue the Ninevites from their troubles. His 'three days and three nights' (a Hebraism to mean 'truly dead') in the whale, followed by new life, was certainly taken by Jesus as a prediction of his death and resurrection (Matthew 12.39–41). Jonah's home village was only three or four miles from Nazareth, so it would be natural, anyway, for Jesus to allude to a local hero!

Despite his death-and-resurrection experience Jonah seems remarkably unrepentant. There is no word of repentance in his psalm, and his attitude has not changed. He is furious when in response to God's reiterated commission he preaches repentance to the Ninevites and the whole city repents (4.1–3). He does not share Yahweh's compassion. He wants to see the city razed to the ground. Not an attractive attitude, and the book of Jonah is designed to show Israel what an ugly and narrow-minded attitude that is.

Thought for the day

God's mercy is greater than I can imagine – even for people I dislike.

Prayer for the day

Lord, when you call me to speak for you in difficult places, may I not run off in the opposite direction but obey your call.

MG

22

Habakkuk: complaint and trust

A prayer of the prophet Habakkuk according to Shigionoth.

O LORD, I have heard of your renown,
 and I stand in awe, O LORD, of your work.
In our own time revive it;
 in our own time make it known;
 in wrath may you remember mercy.
God came from Teman,
 the Holy One from Mount Paran.
His glory covered the heavens,
 and the earth was full of his praise.
The brightness was like the sun;
 rays came forth from his hand,
 where his power lay hidden.
Before him went pestilence,
 and plague followed close behind.
He stopped and shook the earth;
 he looked and made the nations tremble.
The eternal mountains were shattered;
 along his ancient pathways
 the everlasting hills sank low.

I saw the tents of Cushan under affliction;
    the tent-curtains of the land of Midian trembled.
Was your wrath against the rivers, O LORD?
    Or your anger against the rivers,
    or your rage against the sea,
when you drove your horses,
    your chariots to victory?
You brandished your naked bow,
    sated were the arrows at your command.
    You split the earth with rivers.
The mountains saw you, and writhed;
    a torrent of water swept by;
the deep gave forth its voice.
    The sun raised high its hands;
the moon stood still in its exalted place,
    at the light of your arrows speeding by,
    at the gleam of your flashing spear.
In fury you trod the earth,
    in anger you trampled nations.
You came forth to save your people,
    to save your anointed.
You crushed the head of the wicked house,
    laying it bare from foundation to roof.
You pierced with their own arrows the head of his warriors,
    who came like a whirlwind to scatter us,
    gloating as if ready to devour the poor who were in
    hiding.

You trampled the sea with your horses,
    churning the mighty waters.

I hear, and I tremble within;
    my lips quiver at the sound.
Rottenness enters into my bones,
    and my steps tremble beneath me.
I wait quietly for the day of calamity
    to come upon the people who attack us.

Though the fig tree does not blossom,
    and no fruit is on the vines;
though the produce of the olive fails
    and the fields yield no food;
though the flock is cut off from the fold
    and there is no herd in the stalls,
yet I will rejoice in the LORD;
    I will exult in the God of my salvation.
GOD, the Lord, is my strength;
    he makes my feet like the feet of a deer,
    and makes me tread upon the heights.

(Habakkuk 3.1–19)

Is it wrong to argue with God? Job certainly did not think so. Neither did the psalmists. Neither did Habakkuk. But they all did so from a basic position of trust in the God of Israel, their Rock (1.12).

Habakkuk was a contemporary of Jeremiah, and like

him predicted the Babylonian capture of Jerusalem which took place in 587 BC. They saw it as God's judgement on the people's apostasy.

In chapters 1 and 2 Habakkuk raises two vigorous complaints against God. First, why does the evil in Judah go unpunished (1.2–4)? God's answer is that the Babylonians will punish Judah (1.5–11). Habakkuk's second complaint is that the remedy is worse than the disease: how can a just God use wicked Babylonians to punish a people more righteous than themselves (1.12—2.1)? God's answer is that Babylon will in due course be punished and faith rewarded (2.2–20).

Chapter 3 records Habakkuk's prayer. It is more of a psalm, set to music (3.1, 19). The prophet recalls a poetic description of God's mighty acts at the exodus, perhaps one he has heard in the Temple. He is in awe, and begs the Lord to renew his action both in judgement and mercy in his own day (3.2). Actually verse 2 is the only petition he makes, but it is enriched by memories of God's deliverance from terrible situations in the past, supremely the spectacular deliverance of the exodus. Hearing this musical recollection of God's mighty actions of old fills the prophet with such awe that he trembles in physical weakness (verse 16). Despite his complaints against God, he knows God is to be trusted and is therefore prepared to wait patiently for the fulfilment of his promise, the destruction of the Babylonians. This came to pass some 66 years later, in 539 BC.

The prayer (and the book) ends with perhaps the greatest expression of faith in the midst of adversity to be found anywhere in the Old Testament. Habakkuk had stressed in 2.4 that the righteous will live by faith (a complex idea involving both trust in God and the ensuing faithfulness in life). In the final verses of chapter 3 he shows how he is prepared to work that out in his own life: 'Though the fig tree does not blossom, and no fruit is on the vines . . . yet I will rejoice in the LORD; I will exult in the God of my salvation.' Faith in the midst of doubts, joy in the face of adversity – these are the great qualities of the spiritual life which we see in Habakkuk.

Thought for the day

It is all right to complain against God's ways so long as I trust in his faithfulness.

Prayer for the day

Lord, may my faith in you show itself in faithfulness to you.

MG

23

Zechariah: God of the impossible

Then his father Zechariah was filled with the Holy Spirit
and spoke this prophecy:

'Blessed be the Lord God of Israel,
  for he has looked favourably on his people and
  redeemed them.
He has raised up a mighty saviour for us
  in the house of his servant David,
as he spoke through the mouth of his holy prophets
  from of old,
  that we would be saved from our enemies and
  from the hand of all who hate us.
Thus he has shown the mercy promised to our ancestors,
  and has remembered his holy covenant,
the oath that he swore to our ancestor Abraham,
  to grant us that we, being rescued from the hands
  of our enemies,
might serve him without fear, in holiness and
  righteousness
  before him all our days.
And you, child, will be called the prophet of the Most
  High;

for you will go before the Lord to prepare his ways,
to give knowledge of salvation to his people
    by the forgiveness of their sins.
By the tender mercy of our God,
    the dawn from on high will break upon us,
to give light to those who sit in darkness and in the
    shadow of death,
to guide our feet into the way of peace.'

(Luke 1.67–79)

In these last days leading up to Christmas, we are introduced to several people in touch with God but living in very dark times, 'in the days of King Herod of Judea' (1.6) – as bloodthirsty a tyrant as you could find anywhere. They all point unambiguously to God's supreme breakthrough in the person of Jesus and his forerunner, John the Baptist. Not surprisingly, therefore, we meet a concentration of prayer, praise, prediction, prophetic utterance, miracle, the widespread activity of the Holy Spirit and angelic intervention. It is all warming up for the greatest event in world history! Even their names are significant – Zechariah ('the Lord remembers') and Elizabeth ('God is the faithful one'). Gabriel ('man of God', the angel who stands next to God, in 1.19) appears with his joyful message to Zechariah at a highly significant time, as he is making the incense offering in the Temple – a once-in-a-lifetime privilege for a priest. Yes, the drama is about to unfold.

For years, Zechariah and Elizabeth had longed and prayed for a child (1.13), but she was barren and they are both now too old. When Gabriel announces that this oft-repeated prayer is to be answered, and they will have a very special son, Zechariah cannot believe it. So he is struck dumb until the birth, partly as the sign he has requested and partly as a rebuke for his unbelief (1.20). Have you not long prayed for something and then felt incredulous if it was granted?

Nine long months later, Zechariah is fully persuaded that the message of the angel will come true in every part. Hence his firm statement on the writing tablet 'His name is John.' No argument about it! John means 'the Lord is merciful' and that will be the message of the Baptist to those who repent of their self-satisfaction as Israelites and scorn of the hated Roman 'dogs'. As soon as Zechariah expresses his faith, his voice returns to him and he breaks out into the marvellous hymn of praise which we call the Benedictus, from the opening word 'Blessed' in Latin. It is a prophetic hymn of jubilant rejoicing and focuses first on Jesus, the mighty Saviour from the house of David (1.69), bringing to fruition all the prophecies and promises of the Old Testament, particularly the promise God gave Abraham that one of his descendants would bring blessing to the whole world (1.75 – see Chapter 1). Then (1.76–79) Zechariah predicts the unique call on John not only to be the last and greatest of the prophets (1.76, as Jesus called him, in Luke 7.28) but the forerunner of the Lord himself, to prepare his ways by giving 'knowledge of salvation to his people by the forgiveness of their sins'. Only when Jesus, 'the dawn from on high', breaks upon us and assures us of our own forgiveness do we find the way which leads to real peace with God (1.79).

Thought for the day

Time spent alone with God helps us to see clearly.

Prayer for the day

Lord Jesus Christ, make me, like John, someone who prepares the way for others to discover your forgiveness.

MG

24

Mary: joy in the Lord

In those days Mary set out and went with haste to a Judean town in the hill country, where she entered the house of Zechariah and greeted Elizabeth. When Elizabeth heard Mary's greeting, the child leapt in her womb. And Elizabeth was filled with the Holy Spirit and exclaimed with a loud cry, 'Blessed are you among women, and blessed is the fruit of your womb. And why has this happened to me, that the mother of my Lord comes to me? For as soon as I heard the sound of your greeting, the child in my womb leapt for joy. And blessed is she who believed that there would be a fulfilment of what was spoken to her by the Lord.'

And Mary said,

'My soul magnifies the Lord,
　and my spirit rejoices in God
　　　my Saviour,
for he has looked with favour on the
　　　lowliness of his servant.
　Surely, from now on all generations
　　　will call me blessed;

for the Mighty One has done great
things for me,
and holy is his name.
His mercy is for those who fear him
from generation to generation.
He has shown strength with his arm;
he has scattered the proud in the
thoughts of their hearts.
He has brought down the powerful
from their thrones,
and lifted up the lowly;
he has filled the hungry with
good things,
and sent the rich away empty.
He has helped his servant Israel,
in rememberance of his mercy,
according to the promise he made to
our ancestors,
to Abraham and to his descendants
for ever.'

And Mary remained with her for about three months
and then returned to her home. (Luke 1.39–56)

On this Christmas Eve, pride of place must go to Mary and
her wonderful song, which from earliest times has been
sung in the Christian Church. What a woman! She was

probably only a teenager when she received the staggering news that the divine power would come upon her and the child to be born would be called the Son of God. But she was a teenager deeply versed in the Old Testament Scriptures from which almost every phrase of her song, the Magnificat, was drawn and given new significance. Her attitude is one of humble, awestruck acceptance: 'Here am I, the servant of the Lord; let it be with me according to your word' (1.38). What courage! What humility! How would she break the news to her fiancé, Joseph? How would she endure the shame of an apparently illegitimate birth? No wonder Elizabeth exclaimed, 'Blessed are you among women, and blessed is the fruit of your womb.' And 'blessed' the Virgin Mary has been down the centuries. However, in this marvellous hymn of praise there is no trace of pride. She gives no countenance to the idea sometimes put forward that she was immaculately conceived, personally sinless or co-redemptrix. She rejoices in God as her Saviour and glories in the way God has chosen such a lowly person as herself.

The Incarnation launches a powerful revolutionary principle which puts down the proud and exalts the humble and the hungry who yearn for spiritual food. In God's choice of humble folk like Elizabeth and herself, she sees that principle embodied. This great reversal has continued down the centuries; it is one of the glories of our faith that God 'has brought down the powerful from their thrones, and lifted up the lowly'. That principle will be brought to completion at the time of the return of Jesus Christ.

What delightful friendship there must have been between Elizabeth and Mary, both recipients of miraculous pregnancies, both filled with the Holy Spirit. That Spirit enables Elizabeth to recognize in Mary the mother of the promised redeemer whom Psalm 110.1 calls 'my Lord'. She shows no signs of jealousy, but in humility expresses her amazement that the mother of her Lord should visit her and rejoices in Mary's faith that God's promises would be fulfilled (1.45). As we approach Christmas, amid all the pressures of shopping and feasting, these qualities of joy, trust and humility are better decorations than you will find on any Christmas tree!

Thought for the day

As I look forward to tomorrow, my spirit, like Mary's, rejoices in God my Saviour.

Prayer for the day

Lord, please grow in me these beautiful qualities of generosity, love, trust and humility so superbly displayed in Elizabeth and Mary.

MG

25

Shepherds and angels: history's supreme event

In that region there were shepherds living in the fields, keeping watch over their flock by night. Then an angel of the Lord stood before them, and the glory of the Lord shone around them, and they were terrified. But the angel said to them, 'Do not be afraid; for see – I am bringing you good news of great joy for all the people: to you is born this day in the city of David a Saviour, who is the Messiah, the Lord. This will be a sign for you: you will find a child wrapped in bands of cloth and lying in a manger.' And suddenly there was with the angel a multitude of the heavenly host, praising God and saying,

'Glory to God in the highest heaven,
and on earth peace among those whom he favours!'

When the angels had left them and gone into heaven, the shepherds said to one another, 'Let us go now to Bethlehem and see this thing that has taken place, which the Lord has made known to us.' So they went with haste and found Mary and Joseph, and the child lying in the manger. When they saw this, they made known what had been told them about this child; and all who heard it were amazed at what the shepherds told them. But Mary treasured all these words and pondered them in her heart. The shepherds returned, glorifying and praising God for all they had heard and seen, as it had been told them.

(Luke 2.8–20)

Christmas is dismissed by many these days as a fairy story. Far from it. Luke was a careful historian (see Luke 1.1–4) who got his stories of the birth of Jesus and the visit of the shepherds directly or indirectly from Mary herself, when he spent two years researching in Judaea while Paul was in prison in Caesarea. Visions of the angelic choir celebrating the birth of Jesus may seem improbable, but they are nothing compared with the massive improbability of the Creator coming to join his creatures! Though these stories read like a charming idyll, they have the ring of sober historical truth about them – in sharp contrast to the legendary features in the later apocryphal gospels.

Let's allow the stupendous wonder of it to sink in this Christmas day before we get overtaken by the food and festivities. How incomprehensible it would be for a battleship to fit into a bathtub, or a skyscraper into a doll's house. Yet the infinite God took on human flesh and became a baby – laid in a manger! Mary held in her arms the Guest who was the Host of the entire universe. 'God could not make himself any greater to impress us, so he made himself smaller to attract us' (J. John).

On 20 July 1969, Neil Armstrong stood on the moon. President Nixon responded, 'The greatest event in human history occurred when man first put his foot on the moon.' Astronaut James Irwin disagreed: 'The most significant event in our world is not that man stood on the moon, but that God in Christ stood on earth.' That is the meaning of Christmas. It answers the questions 'Who is God?' and 'Where is God?' At Christmas in a humble hovel of poverty and pain, God pulled back the curtains so that we could see his face. And in that life launched on Christmas day we see what God is like. 'He is the human face of God, God's self-portrait,' as Bishop John Pritchard puts it. He is 'a Saviour, who is the Messiah, the Lord' (2.11). He is the Lord who brings the Beyond into our midst. He is the Messiah, the long-awaited prophet, priest and king to whom the whole Old Testament pointed forward.

Moreover, he is the Saviour. We do not so much need a teacher to instruct us or an example to embarrass us, though Jesus is both. We need a saviour to rescue us from our lusts, our fears, our guilt, our addictions. Only Jesus can do that. And when we allow him to be our Saviour he does banish fear and bring joy (2.10). He does bring peace – first peace with God, and then peace given by God through Christ. When that inner harmony is in place, because we are in touch with the Saviour, peace begins to emerge in the welter of our human relations and occupations. The first-century philosopher Epictetus shrewdly commented, 'While the emperor may give peace from war on land and sea, he cannot give peace from passion, grief and envy. He cannot give peace of heart, for which man yearns.' But Jesus can. So this Christmas day let us join the angels and sing in our hearts with joy and adoration, 'Glory to God in the highest heaven' (2.14). Let us also join the shepherds in telling others of the greatest thing in human history, the coming of the Saviour (2.18).

Thought for the day

'The most significant event in our world is not that man stood on the moon but that God in Christ stood on the earth.'

Prayer for the day

Lord, may I today and every day lift my heart to you in adoration for coming to be my Saviour.

MG